SOCIAL MEDIA MARKETING FOR BUSINESS 2020

Your Guide to Branding, Mastery, and Sales with Proven Formulas on Instagram, Facebook, YouTube, and Twitter. Make Money and Accelerate Your Networking Skills

Samuel Smith

Table of Contents

Introduction

Social media (SM) is a paragliding concept that includes the tools and practices people use to exchange views, thoughts, and knowledge among themselves. Even the word is changing. The phrase "social media" most commonly refers to practices that combine technology, social (or human) activity, and text, photos, and audio creations, best known as "user-generated content" [an illustration of UGC will be YouTube videos].

Online networking may take several different forms from communities on the web, weblogs, wikis, podcasts, pictures, and images. Technologies include forums, picture-sharing, vlogs, wall-postings, text, instant messaging, music-sharing, crowdsourcing, and voice over IP, to name a handful.

Examples of social media apps include Google Groups (reference, social networking), Wikipedia (reference), MySpace (social networking), Facebook (social networking), YouMeO (social network aggregation), Last.fm (personal music), YouTube (social networking and video sharing), Second Life (virtual reality), Flickr (photo sharing), Twitter (social networking and microblogging), and other microblogs such as Jaiku and Pownce.

What Is Social Media Marketing (SMM)?

SMM is the medium where you use social media networking and content channels created by users to support a product, service, or material. Typically SMM involves creating and participating in a "conversation" with the target audience, rather than advertising to them blatantly.

SMM can often involve the development and promotion of viral content intended to be posted by users. Many advertisers are not satisfied with the loss of power over social networking, but social networks can be highly powerful platforms for product evangelism, identity building, or corporate branding when properly approached.

How Did They Become So popular?

I just think it's because it mirrors our true nature. By nature we are gregarious, and for once, we can use technology to reach out to effortlessly and communicate in fresh and exciting ways. It's all so new too. There are new frontiers that pop up regularly; it's a bit like the early "gold rush" days of the Internet during the '90s

Is a Social Networking Platform an Entrepreneur's Choice?

Maybe they don't think so but it is. Of course, you already do it every day. SM online is simply the same technologically applied thing.

How Does a Business Owner Determine Which Site Fits Them best?

Good issue. Not all SM places have equal standing. I usually encourage people to talk of "classical ads" and don't let yourself be tricked by the "flashy lights." Join the platform and follow the talk. "Lurking" has been popular for a bit. Ask a comment to see what's going on. Per setting has its own laws. Blunder in and start screaming and you're going to get flamed. Accept the subculture cultures and you'll be doing great. A platform that caters to "gamers" is a clear illustration of this in practice — you immediately realize that if you sold insurance you'd have a rough time in that setting. Think as I said, like a typical marketer.

Are There any "Best Practices" to Start and Maintain the SMM Sites? And How can I Get Social Networking Working for Me?

- The use of Social Networking

  Many a company has forgotten the old maxim, "Act in haste, repent at your leisure..." The same warning should be given to companies rushing to get in on the marketing wave of social media.

  When you say comments like "We can have a forum" at work, or "Let's discuss Twitter," I think [respectfully] maybe you're going to make a whopping error.

Here's why they...

- Backward Is Not healthy

You start planning the social networking campaign backward — so that's going to create problems.

We continue by finding out what we want to do in some other business endeavor. Social networking technology isn't good. They are all instruments too. It's time to avoid selling social networking because it's cool, and do so now because it functions!

Things to Bear in Mind

1. The Internet is for people. Your audience needs to know about you. Understand their online capabilities, hangouts, vocabulary, and behaviors. If you are targeting business travelers then consider, for example, rating and review sites.

2. Find out where the gap would be when you're finished. It's the "why" behind the plans. Would you want a tight-knit group or a testing area for a product? The reason behind the behavior is clear.

3. What outcomes and goals are you looking for? Remember the ultimate result and how you can calculate it. A flippant or fuzzy end product is almost as terrible as not defining one at all. How do you gauge success?

4. Decide which technologies to choose from. Just address this query until the others have been done, and then you will know with certainty and trust.

In conclusion, if among these remarks, you remember traditional principles of business planning and management, you would be right. The game may have changed, but it still has the same rules. Next, prepare and then behave positively.

How long Does It Take To Learn this latest form of Marketing?

The basic skills are pretty easy; you possibly have already learned them. What you need to know about this is the 'method.' It takes a bit of time but not too much honestly.

What if I Don't Realize Why a Ton of People Welcomes Me to My network?

No distress. Answer this question: "If you are the Solution, what was the Problem?" Equipped with that answer, you will identify groups of people that would need what you are selling. You will then encourage them to join and you can SHARE your experience and skills to show you are the solution to their question. To find these people, use your preferred search engine - simply type in the query or problem. Know that, if you knew the answer you wouldn't be asking for it :).

How Can I Get Business Success through SMM?

It's amusing when I'm asked about this. We do it on a daily basis, and I marvel at the fact that online people think it's special. There is definitely a layer of automation in the process, but it is still about having people to know individuals. Remember the old rule, people buy, and trust, people they want.

SMM clearly helps you to do it more easily (or should I say empowers).

A new report from JupiterResearch sheds light on what was suspected for quite some time by many online marketers. Most companies struggle to affect social networks...

Naughton's Law states: "We invariably overestimate the short-term implications of new communications technologies, and we grievously underestimate their long-term impacts." Each brand should be online in the best way, know its consumers, and maximize the benefits of its online offering to those consumers.

Here are some interesting details from the report:

- **Highlights:**

  Only 6,494 friends have a branded social networking page.

  Most companies also establish advertised social networking sites that distribute material rather than allow users to interact with each other.

  "Many marketers just don't know how to target social networks properly." — Jupiter Research

- **New Suggested Research:**

  Instead of focusing on viral marketing to get the news out, you should support the SM sites with paid adverts. It's harder to build up viral hype than you thought.

  Users need to be engaged with the page. Even simple forms of engagement, like contests, have on average doubled the number of friends each branded page has acquired.

You do have to cater to the popularity of social networks to be heard. Social networkers are twice more likely to visit a media content-focused branded page than a product-focused branded page.

How Would this Sort of Advertisement Happen to a non-Writer?

That shouldn't really present a problem. The 'Net' is huge and every one of us has space to be real. Particularly behind a computer's screen, many of us are worthy of sensing a scoundrel or someone "placing on the sand."

If you can give us a text, you can do SM. If you can write, then you can do SM. If there is a heartbeat in you... You get the impression.

Do I Have to Pay Fees to the Social Media Marketing Platforms?

Usually no. I urge you to avoid all places that require payment in the first instance before you know exactly what you are being charged for. There are some decent fee-based places out there, but the good ones always offer a free edition — if you want to start there. Let the findings decide what level of investment you're willing to make.

Are There Certain Places that Business People Can Recommend?

- RelatedIn.com

- Set eCademy.com

- SelfGrowness.com

- Ning.com — create your own website for social media.

Will I have to spend hours a day messaging all the people who write to me?

You'll need to spend energy and time on your online marketing. It's up to you whether it's YOU who does this or one of your employees. But to that which is fundamentally individual, you can't assume a "place and forget" approach.

How Can I Protect Myself against "Weirdoes?"

Be Vigilant. Don't offer personal or sensitive information online. You'll always be introduced to odd people to some degree. I get some very weird emails and ideas, but you need to note that's an industry, and while utilizing "personal skills" to network online, never overlook that.

How Do I Find Myself on these Pages As a specialist, and Should "true" Business Be Conducted that Way?

Publish a Summary by occupation. Display that you're a professional and act accordingly and you'll be seen as such. Take family photos showing you posing as a clown at your own expense during your children's birthday party. Know that the "goofs" are real online and will torment you forever. Online reputation is an environment through which you need to cautiously walk. It's a bit off-topic, but that's why I warn teens to be very cautious about the pictures and updates they place on those social websites. Because in a couple of years the recruiters can search them, and this will be part of their "resume," and honestly, before it even begins, it can be a career killer.

Some people quit too early as with all things in life. It takes time to promote social media and social networking. It's like any partnership you have with another human being — racing to the end always gets you knocked of... metaphorically and also actually!

Online performance is also not about one big thing. It is about a series of little things that are done regularly with commitment and involvement. The best trees grow the fastest. Internet stuff happens even quicker, but there's still a time commitment. Consider 6 to 12 months and you're going to think along the right lines.

There is. Build an employee profile. Publish certain content that will identify you as an expert in your field. The 'readers' must agree and the search engines will accept so. Explore the active or "hot zones" on the SM web. Pay attention to the type of contact and then immerse yourself. Donate first. Create the kudos and credit before trying to ask for anything.

Use technologies to "stream" your SM activity from other places such as your blog or website, to keep up. I use technologies to syndicate and post my content on all my SM pages with the click of one button. It's making it a breeze to link and stay up-to-date.

Try to invite friends to come and visit you. Attach a promotional button on your "other" pages. You should add a "Follow Me" link on your profile, for instance, if you decide to join Twitter! Communicate, communicate, and contribute. Rinse now and repeat.

Rules of Social Media Optimization

Social Media Optimization (SMO) is a series of advertising methods across social media, online networks, and community websites. SMO approaches involve introducing RSS feeds, inserting a Digg or sharing this icon, posting and integrating web third-party apps such as Flickr picture slides and galleries, or YouTube videos. Optimization of social media is a form of marketing through search engines (SEO).

Social media management is related in many respects as a strategy of viral marketing where word-of-mouth is generated not through friends or family but through social bookmarking, video- and photo-sharing platforms through networking. Through sharing content through the use of RSS in the blogosphere and unique blog search engines like Technorati, the interaction with blogs achieves the same in a similar way.

They credited Rohit Bhargava with inventing the word SMO. His original five guidelines for Social Media Optimization have expanded to 16 (as of today). Here's an aggregated list for comparison so far:

1. Greater collaboration

2. Render protocol and bookmarking simple

3. Reward ties come through

4. Support your travel content

5. Fostering mashup

6. Be a customer tool, even if it does not support you

7. Reward respected and supportive consumers

8. Partake

9. Know how to reach the crowd

10. Have content produced

11. Let's be honest

12. Don't think about your origins and remain gracious

13. Don't fear trying new things, keep fresh

14. Establish a plan for SMO

15. Choose the SMO strategies carefully

16. Let SMO be part of your best practices and method

Most of what's mentioned here are common sense; others suggest it's just ads on Web 2.0. If you might think the advice is certainly fine, no matter what, I'm only glad that we are now taking the topic seriously and encouraging the development of strategic content as an essential part of this combination.

Things You Should Learn about Social Networking

1. 3 out of 4 people use the Internet worldwide.

2. Females are an online development sector.

3. 44% of Internet users are between 35 and 54 years of age.

4. Respectively, in North America, 3 out of 4 people use social networks.

5. They invest in certain social networks a total of 6 hours a month and visit more than 800 web pages.

6. 51% of social network users are female — they often consume approximately 200 pages more than men and average 2 hours online.

7. Canada is a country on Facebook, the USA a country on MySpace.

8. 65.7% of Canadians use Facebook per month for a total of 350 minutes and 725 pages of content consumption.

9. The 35+ is Facebook's largest rising age market.

10. In North America, online video and graphics have risen by over 300%.

11. Online videos have an average length of 3.4 minutes

12. Over the last month, 89% of all Internet users viewed a film.

13. YouTube absorbs 57% of all content.

14. Blogs touch over 60% of all North American (online) men. Blogging is increasing at an Internet pace almost double this.

15. North American social networking and a digital touch of more than 80% of the population.

Bottom line: If you're not involved with the customers in social media conversations then you're entering a very uncertain future. As I like to say, "Be Identified, Be Heard, or Be History!"

Chapter 1

What Is Social Media?

Social Media is a red hot buzzword right now, with more than 1,220,000 searches performed for that broad term per month. This means that more than one million people search for something related to social media online each month, whether it's to find a consultant, locate someone who can talk about it with authority, or simply find the answer to the question, "What is social media?"

I aim to answer that question in this essay, in short, easy-to-understand language.

In a nutshell, social media is a way for people to interact using web-based technology. That is to suggest, it's not just one person's publishing details, ever. It's one person's publishing of information in order to get other people to react and interact as a result of that information.

Think about it as starting an Internet conversation rather than delivering an Internet speech in other phrases, more a conversation than a monologue. In comparison to Web 1.0, you might have heard of the term Web 2.0. A Web 1.0 website provides information and content. A Web 2.0 website provides content and information, which allows the reader to engage in the information, vote on the information, and share the information if they wish.

It's all about online interaction with other people. Bearing this in mind, let's look at some examples of the available platforms, including some that may not be so obvious:

- Via Facebook
- Tweet
- Twitch, among other apps for video streaming
- Blogging
- Social bookmarking apps like Digg
- Lines containing notifications
- Customer reviews
- Wike-ups

Both of the websites listed above allow their users to create information on the web and connect with visitors to produce more information.

With over 500 million active Facebook users alone, social media has become a part of the framework of daily life. To place this in context, it would be the third-largest in the world if Facebook were a nation! That means there are more Facebook users in the whole of the United States of America than there are men, women, and children.

Benefits of Social Media

The essay will be about social media today and how it has made other pages become bigger daily. Bigger pages on these social sites tend to use the power of social "knowledge."

So far from social media, I have been able to attract the bulk of traffic, and it was a great starting point to do so. Any new blog would need to draw the advantages of social networking platforms and organize them first.

One of the advantages is the utilization of traffic on the pages already. The ability to attach links on every platform. And then getting to use it if you use every two of the previous items.

With one description of a social network, everyone knows it grows daily. Pinterest: Pinterest. Now technically, it's the "single" biggest social networking platform, also surpassing LinkedIn. It was named, according to Time.com, "50 Best Websites of 2011" and its ranking.

The theme of any social network right now seems to be design visualization. With the illustration of Pinterest as the prime app, the phenomenon has been rising. It's been a phenomenon for bringing the theme into action on Internet dreams.

Social networking has become a major focal point of growth on the Internet in general, as the "person" appears to consider a required dimension of existence in contact with each other.

This book describes the top eight web networks promising advantages. You, too, are taking advantage of the deals on the web network. Check out below and find out the "Benefits!" Share, please!

1. Get fast Traffic

   With Facebook reaching over 845 million active monthly users, at 10 million according to jeffbullas.com and Pinterest, it reveals showing that social networking is one of the Internet's most accessible apps.

   Why not take advantage of the traffic generated by certain social networking sites? Having the traffic and making your brand more "conscious" will be of value to your web.

   Not all of the traffic is what you need. Only a tiny fraction of the numbers. The tiny section that is heavily tailored is what you just want to draw to your website.

   There are other facts on the Internet that are worth taking care of. Of all of them, Facebook is the "Leader" and clearly worth spending time in. It might be special for you, as on Twitter, you could do more talking.

It's more about what time you are spending in a networking network, and the yielding return is dependent on that.

2. Chat and Keep in Touch with Your Peers

   Your colleagues may be site owners or writers who have their material and are delivering it to millions of people. Social networking has rendered partnerships with your peers a probability and "must" type.

   Link and converse with them. That's one of a beginner's most essential things. Simply answering, "Hey, how are you?" is an opening killer to a relationship. Offer also to ask them if any material they have could be shared.

   Having the right top WordPress plugins at your fingertips is one step closer to using social media to the max.

   Ask them individually to ensure that they know that you have posted their material, as they are more likely to respond with the same behavior.

3. Capture a Chase!

Having social media traffic is one thing, but getting them to like you or join you is another. Since social media activity is notorious for traffic that comes and goes, it creates enormous surges and then dwindles the next day.

Half the time a friendly tourist is searching for direction; try the other one to get them to join you. Asking is a start and it is also the start of getting them to sign up to provide unique content.

4. Get more Help with the Web Distribution

Because social media is about interactions and discussing what concerns them most, they might also be interested in posting your article there. They're going to look at it, and what they say could help you continue talking.

One way to have more shares into a piece of content is to include the friends and invite them to distribute it in some way. The other is to email your readers or supporters of "legit" content with whom you are in good connection, and ask them the same way.

5. It's easy Access

There are no costs involved to use them to the fullest extent possible. Create a profile that looks worked on and has all your current "data." Start following and becoming friends with as many of them as you can, and refine your quest gradually.

It is free to share and use the features of the social site, such as meetings or groups. Be aware of the chance to connect with other "similar" people and share what you have to offer. Keep that strategy consistent. They're going to see the rewards.

6. A huge Ideas Database

On social sites, many are looking for answers to their problems in some areas. People are looking for solutions, and one of the places they are looking for is in social media where they might follow one of their teachers, as a blogger or mentor.

Troubles = Ideas. You can also get inspiration by gazing out there at what the theme is and catching some of that feeling. Look at other content and analyze what's getting hits on it for yourself. That is not difficult to figure out. Only look at the social indicators, including feedback or shares, retweets, and so on.

Basically, they spy on your competition.

7. Social Networking = Social Media

Absolutely the fundamental aspect of getting social media success. That, like its other name, could be possible. If on these pages you don't network with others and only pump your own stuff, you can't expect it will be remembered.

Nothing:

The only way it would be is if your fans or those nearby expressed and helped to further support you. I had to know that and didn't think about it that way. So, get in contact with your closest connections and support each other. This way, you can hit the social media channels further down.

8. Increase the "Face" of Your Company

   Only "major" name companies that operated before the hysteria of social media have jumped on this platform to grow their business even further. According to eMarketer.com, 88% of advertisers agree that social media has helped to increase awareness of their brand.

   Even if your website didn't exist before social media, now is the time to grow the site's name into the brand that a larger mass will recognize when it expands. A smart strategy is to look at the big dogs and pick "any" of those tricks they're doing because they have more field experience.

Recap of the eight Advantages of Social Media

There you have it. You can't miss out on social media engagement for the eight huge benefits listed here. It could even be the top 10 advantages of using social media on the website.

No more reasons to not use social networking as it is. Even if you have it, I'm sure you don't take full advantage of it. I did the same before I, too, rediscovered the real essence of social media.

Act one at a time, on each of these eight stages. These are supposed to be functioning points and stepping-stones to the next stage of your interaction with social media.

The real secret to success on every social network is effort and energy, from all these perspectives — time you spend getting stronger at the specific social networking platform.

Why Would Social Networking Ads Be the Subject of any serious Business?

Perhaps we should first determine what precisely social media marketing means before we dive into why. In a nutshell, it involves the combined marketing effort of different models of online social network platform designed to suit your needs. The existing social network sites serve different purposes, and the client or enterprise should therefore be using them accordingly. There's a lot to say about social media marketing, but let's use an illustration to make the argument more poignant.

Using social networking correctly will deliver awesome results, such as when Barack Obama ran for president. Using a properly structured social media marketing plan and supported by Internet marketers who know how to use this powerful weapon, Obama's campaign in January alone earned more than $32 million. After this extremely popular push for social network syndication, Obama's squad managed to reap in February over $50 million without ever holding a single fundraiser.

Yeah, these are massive amounts of money, but to be truthful, a devoted team helped him, all working for one target. With this in mind, it goes to show what you can do if you have a well-considered marketing plan for social media and hire the correct staff member/s to ensure that it is done ethically.

Advantages of Social Media Marketing

Small costs versus large rewards are the main advantages of utilizing social networking. The idea that every organization can create a chart, conduct market analysis, get the word out, do lead generation, or sell a product at such low cost will certainly be a big factor and an incentive to spend time and money in marketing campaigns for social networking.

A huge 85% of Internet marketers have shown that their investments in social media have given substantial attention to their companies. This ties in with the added bonus of acquiring future lifelong faithful customers' all-important eyeballs.

The next best advantage is most definitely Internet traffic and is key to making profits and profitable business connections and alliances like any online business owner know it.

Tribes Promotion

The site today is all abuzz around developing communities and syndicating content on social media with the aim of reaching new consumers. It is recommended that you look at the book *Tribes: We Need You to Guide Us* by Seth Godin. The book focuses on the idea that people will always naturally obey or feel the need to belong to a group that is basically an identification. You will benefit from these ideas as a marketer as you apply these definitions to the business model.

Knowing how to predict consumer behavior would offer every organization greater leverage over other rivals in this cutthroat business climate. Social media marketing isn't just a "fad." It's here to stay, and if you don't know how to use all of these essential social networking resources, the online future may quickly become grim. That is not a strategy of paranoia but simply the plain fact people are pursuing or believing "tribe" stereotypes, and knowing how to exploit this can make the difference between consuming exquisite sauced thick steak or dry bread for dinner.

Playing the game also is the road to prosperity for the social network marketing tribes. Become an engaged community member and offer the kind of content that other participants are searching for and you're going to build a network, reputation, your name, and your website.

Chapter 2

What Is Facebook?

Trends in online media are rapidly evolving. A social networking website is an online forum where users can build a profile that links to other users and express their thoughts. These websites of social networking contain a lot of features that provide avenues for both content evaluation and development. Users share their thoughts, images, perspectives, and news. These websites have traditionally allowed people to stay connected with family and friends, and people with similar interests to share. Worldwide the top four social media networks are Facebook, Linked-In, MySpace, or Twitter.

Facebook is a wonderful forum, indeed. It's becoming an extremely important online communications platform. It's quickly turning into another kind of advertisement and engagement and ads for several companies around the world. It is an ever-expanding means of online networking and engagement. Facebook is certainly a Web platform of the Internet that helps users to exchange messages.

Billions of people around the world use this forum but only a few people know how to use this website properly. Facebook is also a common online networking program that helps people to exchange information with others. It's an important tool for advertisement and promotions, enabling products and companies to stay in contact to support them. Complementing the internet marketing approach is a great website and advertisement tool. It's an absolutely free approach, perfect for selling your services and goods as an online platform. Consequently, Facebook has become an advertisement and promotion tool for easily targeting a common target consumer. Now it's a common subject for online social marketing. It's an outstanding training forum for educators.

Facebook helps users to put their views anonymously. It's a lot safer for organizations because it helps you to acquire information from communities that you wouldn't necessarily be open to, otherwise. It's used by all, not just leaders of the Athletic People, Authors, Actors, and Organization. It's the transparent forum for social networking; here users will genuinely tell you about your goods and services. It is a continuous pulse element which means your attention span can really fly. It is best for making a sensation about a successful project kick-off or an aggressive product or service advertising and marketing. It is ideal for the delivery of your services or goods. It is the ideal location at this time to sell your services or goods or the web, as it is very sunny.

Facebook is a social networking site that functions in fact similar to MySpace or Twitter. It's similar to blogging while MySpace or Facebook blends with the whole online culture. Facebook is just a social networking platform where family members, acquaintances, groups, co-workers, or people with the same tastes and hobbies are held linked. It's been a huge part of my connection with my former colleagues, my customer base. It was really available, and I didn't have any issues with the services Facebook provides.

How to Use Facebook for Business

Companies are gradually utilizing a variety of social networking platforms in their marketing activities. The trick to making successful use of social media is not to be anywhere, but to create an online presence where the existing and prospective clients are online. Contrary to what others believe- Facebook is not either for students in college or for personal use. Companies are constantly utilizing Facebook in a range of innovative ways, such as creating their brand identity, pushing traffic to their website and forums, revealing or collecting input on new items, maintaining their online credibility, recruiting staff, sharing client details, and intercepting future outlooks. This improved client contact contributes to strengthened partnerships with existing and potential clients for several businesses. In this book, I will explain how a prepared approach to internet marketing will deliver good results for your company. I'll continue the book by answering a few growing misunderstandings regarding Facebook that I hear most often from my customers.

Next, I'll explain how the various parts of a Facebook account should be used and set up. I'll conclude with a range of suggested applications that attach features to your Facebook company account.

Misconception #1: *Facebook is for personal usage only*

Any time I offer presentations on using social networking platforms for the company, there is the audience's impression that Facebook is only useful to connect with friends and relatives. Facebook launched as a closed network for college students and was not as good at showcasing the company page and ads functionality as LinkedIn had. Facebook, though, continues to grow in use among businesses seeking to reach more than 200 million active users and has very strong and tailored targeting tools that help marketers zero in on their target market.

Growing misconception #2: *Facebook is for pupils only*

According to the Facebook Press Room website, Facebook has more than 200 million active users and a million new members enter the U.S. alone each week. About two-thirds of Facebook users are not in a class, contrary to what many of my followers say. More than 50% of Facebook users in the U.S. are over 35 according to comscore.com; the single-largest population category in the U.S. on Facebook is currently between 35 and 44, while the highest rising age segment of Facebook is 55 and over. They also announced that Facebook ranks in most European countries as the highest social networking platform.

Growing Misconception #3: *I'm too tired, and anyway, my time isn't worth it.*

Some of the reasons companies are increasingly utilizing social networking sites like Facebook are because they provide businesses with the opportunity to connect with people in their network regularly, easily, and efficiently. Networks can include companies they already do business with, people they want to do business with, suppliers, and potential business partners.

Social networking sites such as Facebook act as an alternative to traditional means of communication such as newspapers and direct mail, and in some instances, as a substitution. Facebook can be used to launch or seek feedback on new items regularly, to showcase new employees or current staff accomplishments or abilities, to encourage customer loyalty, to advertise special events and special offers, and to create partnerships. According to an immersive online marketing study survey conducted by Forrester Research (March 2009): "40 percent of the companies surveyed plan to curb direct mail expenses, while 35 percent would decrease newspaper advertising, and 28 percent would slash magazine money to spend more on interactive media." Several companies have reported that using these electronic means of communication has decreased the amount of money they spend.

Which Social Web Works

What companies use social networking sites found is that these sites allow them to connect more frequently with individuals, vendors, customers, peers, and prospects, which in turn helps businesses better understand their customer needs, increase trust, and thus build better business relationships. Most people know that Facebook acted as a platform to link or re-connect with friends, family, and colleagues. And most realize that even personal connections can become new business opportunities — so it makes sense to use Facebook to communicate with those in the business environment.

How to Setup Facebook Profile

You need to create an account to allow the use of Facebook. You need to do the following upon registration to be of importance:

1. *Create a Portfolio/Profile*

   To start using Facebook you need to build a profile detailing your own information. You may build just 1 profile based on the site rules, and it must be related to individual identity, ideally your real name, not a business name. Later in this book, we will discuss the setting up of your business page, but first, you need to set up your profile. Using your maiden and husband names if you are a married woman so that more people can find you. Facebook has a "Friend Finder" feature that enables users to search for individuals through education, business, or organization. So you must be sure to list all of your previous schools, organizations, jobs in your profile in order for people to find you. Complete the section entitled "About Me" to explain your company and what services or products you deliver. You will need to include links to your website address, email, journal, and other business information such as your company's contact information, logo, and a picture of yourself in the "Profile" box on your profile page. You should find your profile page as your "branding" account or your marketing campaign. If you're working for a company you don't have to mention all of your personal interests — just restrict your application to listing your business interests. Your article can be syndicated on your profile page. By doing so, you allow any post you make to appear automatically on your profile page and all those people who are associated with you will see it.

2. *Create Your Contact List*

Facebook was created with the idea of connecting with friends. You can send and receive "friend requests" and your friend will be able to view your profile if approved, and you can see theirs. You can either import your address book/contact database or start connecting with people you know, or you can even check for specific people on Facebook.

You can also show each user you are linked to on the friends' list. If you know any of the contacts your new friend has, or you want to learn them, you can send a request for a link. By welcoming all of your customers, business partners, vendors, family, friends, colleagues, school graduates, neighbors, and anyone else you think would be interested in connecting, you will expand your friend list. I would also consider using the Facebook search function to look up people you've lost contact with. Your profile should appear on all the profiles of your friends after being nice. Therefore, the more followers you have, the more sites your profile seems to contribute to more users viewing your account and potentially coming into contact with you.

3. *Communicate via Wall Posts*

Any member of Facebook has a "bar," where friends can post messages. This is the electronic equivalent of calling them on the phone, in the business networking environment. Through writing this on your screen, posting about the latest service or product launch, or sharing a forthcoming training or networking event, you will give a compliment to a colleague regarding their job.

4. *Update Your Status*

A status box lies at the top of your Facebook account. Everybody on your contacts list will see your message on their site anytime you add a status change. This is the place to exchange advice for company owners, advertise activities, post blog posts, introduce new items, links to your partner services, links to fun video or audio videos, directories, articles, and newsletters. You can attach reminders as much as you do in the "What's on you?" tab.

This should show on all the accounts of your contacts and make sure they're supposed to be on your contact list with others and are competent in nature. Otherwise, you're losing people getting you off their list.

5. *Partake in online Forums*

Online communities let you remotely network with potential customers and peers. You will even enter groups related to your job on Facebook. There are therapy classes, students, coaches, and any possible occupation. You will network, and benefit from in-field experts. Another means of leveraging such groups' capacity and importance is to create one of your own. There are no expenses for doing so and this is a perfect way to increase the exposure of the business. I launched a forum for the managers of behavioral health services in Boston, for example. This community is now a tool for exchanging best practices, which will contribute to relationships of shared understanding over time. Starting from your Facebook home page to join groups, view the membership list, and click on "Groups." You will search through thousands of groups by area of interest, by sector, and by geography. All over the world, there is an incredibly varied range of topics and occupations.

6. *Create a List of Your Friends*

It makes sense to get as many mates as possible, for business purposes. One way to do so is to enter a community and submit requests for contacts to fellow participants with a note reminding them of your value in talking to them on Facebook. Just as you would for an introduction to an in-person company, be sure to check out their profile and learn what they are currently doing. Networking also functions well where a two-way exchange takes place. Find opportunities to support them by exposing them to a friend or future business associate and they are likely to reciprocate and return their favor. Also, make your own events page, or add an "events page" on Facebook. You can even see how many RSVPs there are and get feedback from the participants.

7. *Creating Sites for Fans*

Since Facebook needs the assignment of a profile to an individual, not a company, instead they have given the option to build fan pages. For a company, book, drink, blogger, speaker, celebrity, or just about everything else you want you can build a fan page. To build a fan page, scroll down to the bottom of Facebook and click on "Advertise" (do not worry, the configuration is free). Next, press at the top of the computer on "Pages." You'll find some useful examples of how pages function, along with the connection that allows you to create your fan page. You may add links, activities, discussion boards, and other features to render them social once your page is developed. Your fan pages posts should show on your profile and your mates will be informed of them. You should invite people to become a "fan" of your website as an alternative to sending requests for friends that will help you to build an online community

8. *Using the Mercado*

Facebook has an online marketplace that lets you list your products and services at no discount. This is a great way to get an audience for you or the client. You can also check the internet for items or services you need.

How to Set Up a Facebook Business Page

A business page is easy to set up. Only sign in to your profile page and scroll down the screen at the edges. Then click on "Advertise" or by following this link:

http://www.facebook.com/business

This will pull up a website with the blue links one of which is named "Pages." Click on Pages, then click on the green "Build a Profile" box on the right of the computer. Now you can start filling in this information to create and configure your company page.

Facebook can immediately add an application named the "Domain Admin" when you build your business account, which will be found at the top and left side of your file. Again choose Facebook Pages, then choose the best category for your business. To load your business page, click this button, where you can then modify and connect to the existing material.

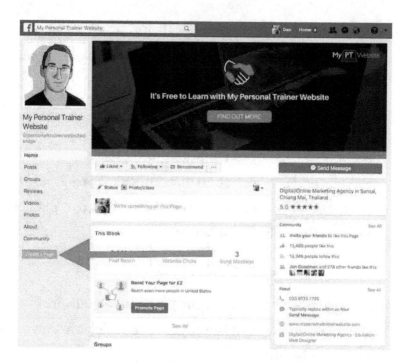

It is crucial that you carefully choose the name of your Facebook page since the name of the page would become your keyword search words, which is the only text included in a Facebook page search. Once your page is in place, you can add applications that help to promote your specific way of portraying your business. Click on "Applications" in the upper left corner of the page to find applications for Facebook, or check for them in this link:

http://www.facebook.com/apps

Applications are fairly easy to install and set up. If you have difficulty with any program — please note that there is always more than one application available to perform the same task.

Google Business Apps:

- **Simply RSS:** This allows you to display up to eight RSS feeds on your Facebook page and show the feeds from the main website and newsrooms of your company.

- **Upcoming:** Submit all the activities to upcoming.org, and you can conveniently view them with the Upcoming Facebook application on your Facebook page.

- **My Flickr:** Use this program to display photos from your Flickr page. Such pictures can include labels, product pictures, event pictures, etc.

- **Added Things pro:** Helps you to add numerous YouTube, Yahoo, and Google Photos, mp3 songs, blogs, links, and more on your Facebook and Twitter pages. Any number of these features can be incorporated, making it great for a media center or press segment.

- **Twitter APP:** If you have a Twitter account, this program will instantly drag your messages into your Facebook status and add a Twitter-themed icon that will let all of your Facebook friends realize you're on Twitter. It also saves uploading time and makes sure you have some profile behavior to keep you interested. If you're not on Twitter yet-at any point you should add this.

By integrating these applications, you can build an engaging website that will offer visitors a deeper understanding of your market.

To remain important on Facebook, you need to update your Account constantly and use the app. If you can't do this regularly — then I would recommend you employ a copywriter or expert on social media to help. The more acts you take, the more in the News Feed of a fan that you show. This holds you in mind while they communicate with you, and in feeds from their mate. But posting posts would do more than just hold you on the News Feed; it would also help make your Facebook Profile something that users can come back to by giving fans an opportunity to start reading your articles and subscribing to your website. This can be done in many ways, such as offering unique material, exclusive promotional pricing, exclusive competitions, product demos, or privileged access to company events.

I hope you've found this information helpful in getting started using Facebook. Don't make any mistake about it-social networking isn't a fad. Google is here to live, and other social media sites. And irrespective of whether you're using all the social networking sites, you can't discount recent research finding that consumers are increasingly online to gather information regarding companies and products, compare prices, and place orders. As for all emerging technology, social networking can require time and energy for companies to take full advantage of it; nevertheless, I agree that this time and effort would be well invested if achieved regularly and in a prepared, careful manner.

Increasing Your Podcast Downloads Using the Facebook Algorithm to Your Advantage

If you're focusing on increasing your interactions in these areas, you will increase your overall "algorithm score" and see more of your posts being promoted to a broader public.

I use this method to help boost the number of downloads I get and my podcast shows. I've seen an increase in the number of views my podcast has earned over time by using Facebook to share the information (as opposed to when I don't talk about an episode).

But just posting a link to your podcast episode won't do much to help. You need to make the Facebook algorithm's full spectrum analysis and use it to your advantage. It is probable, and the details below will aid in this field.

First is the number of comments you get on a post or photo, and you like them. With posts from other users, you will increase this amount by more. This means they almost always do the same for your posts.

In reality, the next field is "engagements." How many pages and posts of your peers are you posting on and engaging in conversations. Not just giving a "Like." But conversations.

That leads us to "Replies." You need to reply with feedback on your articles to raise the engagement score (which derives from comments and likes). You'll be surprised at the number of interactions you'll have if you do. Concerning Facebook, each of these conversations is "extra points."

Remember Facebook is a platform for social media. Everything is designed to communicate. Not just self-promotion. The stronger the algorithm ranking would be, the more you communicate with others. The amount of articles you send isn't too many. This is about how many others you communicate with.

That gives to the shares. How many updates do you exchange with other users? What's more, how many people read your content? In the algorithm, the shares rank better than Likes. So the better the ranking the more Shares you have.

Is it the same for two or three individuals who share your posts? Or get the same material posted by the same pair of friends. When you post information from someone who already scores high on the algorithm (a well-known celebrity in your niche), the algorithm would award bonus points.

Hand in hand with that is the content's generation. The daily Facebook post is around 4-5 hours of real-time. So if someone shares your articles 12 hours ago (or longer), the algorithm doesn't assign the share as much importance as if they posted something about 1-2 hours ago. The more recent the post, and the higher the ranking for that post, the more shares you get.

It is necessary to post material from algorithm two or three days earlier and continue to earn bonus points. How? How? In addition to the post's era, the algorithm often considers the period that has passed after the most recent posting or message. And if you always get feedback, like, tweet, respond and share two, three, or even a week later, that post gets a higher score than others. Facebook will proceed to view the post further down your friend's list.

Next, is the software posting system. Is it a mobile phone or a laptop computer? Sure, you can tell the difference with the Facebook algorithm! Those who use the app from their smartphone are getting higher scores in this day and period than those who just use Facebook from home (after work and at the end of the day). Smartphones make access during the day, and Facebook needs that!

The Facebook algorithm also looks at the type of post it is creating. Is it all text? Have that included a video or an image? Is that just a video? Are ties to other Facebook accounts or profiles still included? Was it a picture on Facebook Live?

Facebook is now also pushing their live stream. When you decide to film and share a video on YouTube, use their Facebook Live to do so. It'll easily be posted on Twitter. Live video scores algorithmically strong. A video can scores higher than a photo or photograph. Yet it's far easier to get a photo than merely a text message.

Another way to increase the ranking on your algorithm is to "tag" other users anytime you write, comment, or retweet a message. You immediately inform them of the article by 'tagging' them. Typically that will include them viewing the article and returning comments. Remember, it is the interaction that the algorithm is monitoring!

Look out for connections that keep users off Facebook (such as a link to your website or YouTube). Facebook will cut the code ratings drastically. Now, people want to live on their boards. Place the connection on a post on a blog if you just need to add a link to a website etc. Using the key article instead to bring users over to your Facebook account.

One approach used (and Facebook is heading towards tracking now) is to place the answer in the first comment down below the message. You post and then say something like, "for a guide, please look at the message below." So you "heart" the article and make a page for people to read that contains the connection to your website (or elsewhere).

Facebook is "moving to" this process, so it reduces the number of posts doing this. It works better if you have two or three comments and replies and make the link. Yet there is already something that's going to reduce your average post ranking. Note, Facebook is eager to have you on their website.

Another field where the algorithm tracks are how long people spend on your message. Do they display it in a scroll? They are waiting, pressing the button, and then going on? Or do they sit there, read the content, write a comment, post it, and communicate with others? Will they waste many minutes there? On the algorithm, that'll score high.

The algorithm should also take the fullness of the profile into account. Have you just posted the most basic information, or are almost all areas completed? Have you ever seen Facebook give you notes of "adding a telephone number" or "adding an address" to your page so that more users might "search you?" This is not about people calling you at 2 am. It's about the Facebook algorithm which exposes you to more users. (But be sure not to mention your personal address and mobile or cell number on a Facebook profile. I use your work address and company telephone number-if necessary)!

The Facebook algorithm gives each individual his or her own, personal "performance." The algorithm continuously changes this score in special to all and every individual. You may have a low score right now but the connections you'll create on the Facebook site over the next few hours raise that. So, when you shut down Facebook for the day and go to bed, go to work, or even go out for a few hours, it continues to fade.

The more time you spend on the website, and the better the algorithm ranking would be, the more you communicate with others. The more Facebook supports your profile and updates, the higher your ranking. The lower the score, the less the amount of your friends who see your messages.

I hope this information provided you a better insight into how the Facebook algorithm works. All of these variables in the Facebook algorithm, labeled "Signals," are modified constantly and almost instantaneously. Use this knowledge for your gain and you'll reap the benefits! The Facebook algorithm will share your posts analyzing your podcast episodes widely and in detail!

What Makes Facebook Advertising Different?

Google may have gained more money in the past but they are overtaken by Facebook. It's clear that Facebook uses a different advertising strategy than other sites.

Let's take a deeper look at what makes Facebook ads special, and why they rapidly produced overtime of 500,000,000 registered users surpassing existing advertisement firms. Why is Facebook a hazard as an entity winning supremacy?

Facebook uses social graph or activities to target individuals. On the other side, Google helps users to place their needs or to guide them through different words or queries.

While ads pay for advertisements, Facebook advertisement is special in that it helps advertisers to consider their target. At the time Facebook incorporates the desires and preferences of users. Google uses keywords, instead.

There's a big gap 1:20 at the expense of utilizing Facebook versus Google that an advertiser has. Fancy the money.

Along with marketers, Google depends on keywords that are a measurable activity for drawing an audience. Many Facebook users are registered and genuinely have qualitative details regarding them which Facebook then uses to help marketers reach their potential audiences.

Since Facebook audience provides information about their interests, and advertisers can offer a product that matches them readily, advertisers can then effectively sell their product with fewer clicks, resulting in lower costs. On the other side, Google's ads are search-based and users need to enter keywords in the search box and perform a number of searches before the ad shows up.

In comparison to what Twitter does, Google uses Search Ads which is Flash Advertisement. Google helps a consumer to check for keywords and Facebook links the keywords to the preferences and desires of an individual and shows these stand-out advertisements in front of the customer.

Yes, you may not really find well-targeted AdWords on Facebook but you will always find a tailor-fitted advertisement at the sidebar. Advertising on Facebook is special since it utilizes simple data to selectively target a single person.

Google is created into a pay-per-click advertisement (PPC) so that the advertisement can only be viewed once when the search engine is used. For Facebook, on the other side, there is a temptation for people to go blindly into advertising and as a social networking platform, people may constantly see the commercial, and marketers need to build or develop more ads or adjust their ads several times.

These may be certain categories were ads on Facebook do not function, but in fact, it is really successful for other users because it is specifically tailored and marketers can have the specific form of customers clicking on their advertisements. This innovative promotional approach is achieving strong numbers and a fresh interest for consumers and marketers alike.

What Is Instagram and Why Is Instagram So Important for Your Personal and Company Brand?

Many citizens have already learned about Instagram's tiny feature, which has taken the globe by storm. If you're a development specialist, understanding the new and best software, it doesn't matter, if you can barely search your inbox. We will both rely on Instagram being just somebody we know. It's a remarkable sight if you turn around today that you don't see anyone stuck to their screen, completely oblivious of what's going on around them. How much people use their phone while in the middle of a conversation is really fascinating, sometimes more focused on the screen than the interaction they have with the person right in front of them. Has anything ever occurred to you, or maybe you have also done it yourself?

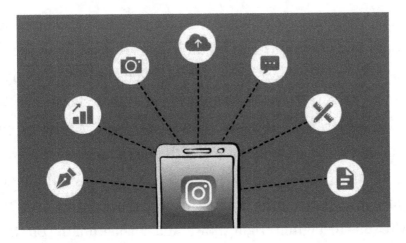

It is a new climate in which we work now; as compared to 10-20 years ago. Until then, computers weren't that clever, applications just weren't as common, so people still haven't been utterly obsessed with their gadgets, and more especially, the software they're using. Nowadays, you can use apps such as Instagram to chat with friends whether by including them in something you saw, sending them a video message, referring to a story they shared, or even seeing something that reminded you of it. You may even get caught visiting various towns, experiencing real life from your favorite celebrity, or performing live steam from last night's game with your favorite comic or any sports highlights. None of this existed fifteen years ago, people back then could turn to the Television for television, but now people spend more time on their phones than ever before, and Facebook is where they spend much of their time. Whether you own a company or want to build your own personal brand... Instagram is one of the sites you ought to use, and here's why.

Do you think you have exposure to more than 800 million people a month on Instagram? Instagram is quickly growing to the top of all social networking sites and it has been one of the strongest channels for targeting the target market with a staggering 800 million subscribers. Though Twitter has been sitting at 350 million users for a couple of years, Instagram has shot beyond that, hitting 1 billion users over the next year or two. As the old slogan goes, "To reach the clients and people where they are." And they're on Instagram right now, and Instagram is on their computer to make it much more effective. Look about and you will still see somebody looking at their screen, and particularly using Instagram.

Instagram allows things easy for you to network. The networking features and vast scope Instagram has provided us are unrivaled on a global scale. Smart people like you realize that they have to take every chance to develop and extend their network. Instagram allows you to communicate with people based on their likes, location, hashtags, and friends and interactions with one another. The best aspect of this is that you can develop your network from your mobile around the globe. So that really offers you a legitimate excuse to waste all the time on Instagram.

Instagram maximizes interaction and scope. Instagram has 58 times more scope and participation to track than Facebook, and an astounding 120 times greater coverage than Twitter. Creating your Instagram following is, therefore, crucial to your performance now, and more so in the future. If you don't develop a target market (people involved in a company or personal brand) so it's more like you don't have a mobile phone or email for people to reach you. It's like a fisherman who doesn't have a fishing pole or net to catch fish, a barber who doesn't have clippers for hair cutting, we're sure you get the point right now. Start building your audience today so you can continue gaining momentum and recognition rapidly setting up yourself with a strong foundation to build on for the future.

Instagram is enjoyable and user friendly. For those acquainted with Instagram, you probably know how enjoyable and user friendly it is. You presumably also realize how effective Instagram can be if you already have a personal or a company page. Users will visit various towns, countries, and continents straight from their phones and display and do live videos with their viewers as well. You will engage in a live video, interview style with someone. And with new functionality always introduced, the possibilities are infinite. Instagram helps you to essentially get your own TV network without the TV network bill. Far better you can get live feedback from your listeners with the correct feedback and interaction when you speak to them, that's more important than TV.

People now and always enjoy photos and always have and always will. For those who've never used Instagram before, it can be a perfect way to connect with people and create a highly focused, targeted audience. Based on your preference; company, careers, or interest you will create an audience that is local, national, or international. There's an old saying, "A photo is worth a thousand words." Begin using Instagram now, and let your photos teach you a thousand words. For centuries people have always taken photos and you know Instagram would be going for the long haul.

Instagram allows you to create meaningful connections. By now, most people know that Instagram is growing by leaps and bounds. The timing is now right for you, particularly in the last several years. Everyone knows someone who is always checking their Instagram on their phone, and more importantly, Instagram holds the attention of the people. It has become one of the best forums people and businesses can use to communicate with others. Could you imagine just using Instagram to connect with new users and potential customers every day? What if you built a warm, important, link to your audience? At the same time create and develop your own brand and presence in people's minds around the globe. Not to mention keeping up-to-date with friends and relatives, Instagram really helps you to do that and more.

Building your audience on Instagram is crucial but expanding your own Instagram is challenging with the ever-changing algorithm. This helps the account expand much faster. You can post content on a daily basis and you may not see the type of growth you'd expect.

Instagram Marketing Tips for Your Business

Millions of people worldwide use Instagram today. Instagram has made taking pictures easy and posting them with friends and many people enjoy doing that. Including networking, you can use Instagram for ads in a more efficient way. Instagram is a great promotional tool that you can use to promote your online business.

Tell the Story through Pictures and Videos

Photos are worth a thousand words and pictures are all about Instagram. If you are on Instagram for marketing purposes then you should realize that spontaneous pictures are not effective. You need to continually post photos of your items. Posting images of your products is one of the best ways to increase awareness of your brand and to boost sales of your products. The images needn't necessarily be very professional. The key thing is to have the pictures show the principal characteristics and functions of the products that you endorse. The pictures on Instagram should appeal to vast audiences.

Instagram ads, videos are critical too. To advertise the commodity at hand, you should create and post a video with your employees. You can also choose to do and post a live video review of the product on Instagram. Photos and videos are more enticing to others than text files. Media files are most apt to go viral because users upload them. Also, they are more unforgettable than text archives. Create photos and videos that show the story and the values of your brand. So if you want to boost your brand and revenue, the photos and videos are relevant.

You need to make and share high-quality photos and videos on your feeds to improve your visibility. Request professional help or advice from a photographer where necessary. You can take clear pictures using a decent camera though. Seek to get your photos in the best possible positions. For better outcomes edit your pictures. Nowadays for this reason mobile phones are fitted with photo editing software. Instagram has several resources for uploading images too. Using these resources for marketing purposes on Instagram.

Sign in with Followers

Maintaining communication with your customers is crucial particularly for the growth of small market share businesses. You should start by showing your customers how serious you are about their reviews. You will do this by addressing their questions and comments. This will boost the quality and popularity generated by users, as well as increase the exposure of your products and business. The success of your business can be significantly influenced by your Instagram followers and you should never neglect them.

Use Hashtags

Hashtags are important in marketing on Instagram. You need to use them because we use hashtags to communicate with Instagram users. Hashtags allow users to search for your content and are relevant if you want to maximize your followers. Has media-like tags will create a viral effect that benefits your company. Trending hashtags can also be used especially if the hashtags are related to your product. This is significant since users of Instagram can search for posts using hashtags.

Using Hashtags for Brand Name

You should have your business name inside your hashtags. For a particular promotional campaign you are running, use unique hashtags. This not only highlights the initiative but also offers your members a specific hashtag to connect and share with other partners.

Have a friendly attitude towards all

You need to recognize that Instagram is a culture made up of people with varied ideas, feelings, and experiences when conducting Instagram marketing. Please be polite to others, and appreciate their time on your website to interact with you. Just make sure the consumers listen.

Stay active

Write at least once a day to bring it up-to-date and to ensure that your fans are updated with the latest events. You should try posting to see which time the posts perform well at different times of the day.

Cohesiveness

Consistency is crucial in marketing on Instagram. Be consistent in your posts, and establish a popular trend in your posts. Let the fans exactly what to expect of you.

To boost your marketing ability link your Instagram and Facebook accounts. Nowadays you can provide your Facebook page with an Instagram link. When you have a fan page, this allows you to share your Instagram posts with your Facebook followers.

Using Instagram to network with peers and the planet. May use Instagram for marketing purposes. Marketing with Instagram will boost the visibility of your brand, increase sales, and ultimately revenues. Find the above marketing tips for performance with Instagram.

The Path to Instagram Analytics with Measurements and Observations

As a social media platform, Instagram is an enormous sensation. Photo uploading, video uploading, live videos, geolocation, hashtag stream, several image update, DM functionality updates, Instagram account stickers and polls, and a whole new batch of innovative web apps are introduced to the framework rather frequently.

Restricted to being just a smartphone app and a simple website, Instagram has risen as one of today's most commonly used and enjoyed social apps.

Having said all of this, the Facebook SDK redesign and improvements to the Snapchat API are just as much thought about. Exasperation spread everywhere among brands and marketers after updates to the Instagram API have been published. Brands and third-party developers were subject to stringent rules and regulations and had to comply with the API upgrade.

Check Links to Instagram API Before and After

Before the Instagram API was launched, businesses had to display metrics through insights into the application. Although, on the latest API framework which is better fitted, analytics insights can be obtained now.

It will now be easier to track the success of organic content on third-party tools with this API as it is now focused on the same methodology as the Facebook Graph API.

The new metrics and insights will empower businesses to stay ahead in the race for their organic content performance over what they had previously been receiving with third-party tools.

Why Do I Need Reports and Insights on Instagram?

Instagram analytics is an important component of Instagram marketing strategies. Marketing efforts by marketers will lead to a waste of money and resources without accurate reporting on analytics. Analytics help to determine how large the marketing strategies are. In order to enhance efficiency and approach to marketing and advertisement materials, it is simple to monitor which outcomes are obtained after the implementation of the marketing strategy, etc.

With the latest Instagram API update, company success on Instagram can easily be decoded with Instagram analytics.

The Task for Tracking Material

The redesign of the Instagram API includes a new feature that allows businesses to limit and regulate information. Companies can use this function successfully to cover feedback in the light of organic content. It means that a balanced forum is preserved to express thoughts, as a flexible option to view or not to show feedback and move between them.

In addition to this feature, an automated system also detects offensive and commentary-provoking comments and helps businesses to moderate their content.

Business Profile Compatibility with the Instagram API Update

To use the Instagram API update, a company profile on Instagram would be needed now. The newly released API also requires a Facebook login for the use of third-party tools.

Existing API resources can be used and used by businesses, but the benefit of using the new features does not come with this. In fact, signing in to Facebook will be a prerequisite for this.

Instagram Beta As Server for Facebook Graph

Google contains numerous valuable changes to its Graph API that includes:

- The data can be obtained from 140 million places worldwide.

- Greater metrics of engagement to any URL.

- To support calls to the Read-After-Write API.

- Updated endpoint insights page.

- A new endpoint of the API is built to link a Facebook customer to their Messenger Bot easily from the brand's application.

- Multiple features are designed to leverage marketing API power.

- Video API with cross-post endpoints for the images.

- Online connect alerts, the subscription-based push program for applications offered by Facebook.

- Instagram API can test the stats and observations

Instagram provides an array of indicators and data for marketers and companies to evaluate their efficiency, compare and assess their objectives and outcomes, identify customer feedback and preferences and then make improvements in their marketing strategy accordingly.

Brands can monitor reach, interactions, saves, and video and profile views for individual posts.

Brands will monitor departure levels, views, page visits, scope, comments, and feedback from users in stories. Instagram stories are a new approach that helps advertisers monitor efficiency.

Brands will map outage, class, top locations for the audience. Age and ethnicity are common details for every social media that is requested.

Despite Instagram changing the platform and use API, it is getting important for marketers to conform to it for a profitable market with the day that passes.

How to Build Real Followers on Instagram

The best way to grow your company using this powerful brand, marketing tool for viewers and content

Lately, we spoke with Instagram on how to improve your company marketing. Contrary to what many people mistakenly say, Instagram is not just a nice platform where you can share photos of food, holidays, and relatives.

Instagram has become a popular tool for companies to build brands, develop markets, and sell material. It has over 200 million active monthly members who post 60 million photos, and 1.6 billion likes a day.

A note of caution: there are plenty of people out there promising to expand your thousands of Instagram followers but lookout. Most use bots created fake accounts to inflate your numbers.

These followers' forms have a null value. They can actually even be dangerous, wanting to steal your password or pictures or infect you with a virus.

Such evil bots account for 28.9 percent of bots on Instagram, according to cyber protection company Imperva.

Being true to your company is the perfect way to create your Instagram followers.

Here are 3 suggestions to help you bring real followers on Instagram:

1. Hashtag Stories

    Use a brand name as a symbol is fantastic but you have to look at that.

    When you choose to attract fans for your Instagram images, using those hashtags that say the tale of the picture you're posting. When sharing posts for stuff like: You want to start a conversation.

    - Reviews
    - Highlights
    - Concussions
    - Product entrepreneurs

    @Tostitos is a perfect example of a brand that does this well. We are now using the hashtag # GetTogether to inspire people to come together and exchange their chips, and even to use the hashtag when uploading photos of their meetups.

You will discover yourself in Instagram searches by using entertaining, appropriate hashtags, and hopefully, build up followers on Instagram.

2. Gain imagination

    Instagram is just about videos, and many users talk after-thought of the caption.

    Don't forget the caption for the pic! By using descriptive words that will engage, inspire, and entertain your followers, you can generate engagement and promote sharing.

    Below are a few tips to help you create up Instagram followers for your posts:

    - Using the caption to raise questions. Write down your question at the start of the post so people see it first.
    - Get the post personalized. Say a tale about yourself, or about anyone else supported or influenced your idea.
    - Ask others to tag. Asking users to add three of their closest mates or adding someone they are thankful for getting into the mix certain future followers.

    The @NatGeo Instagram account is a perfect example of a brand that does custom content well.

They produce stunning Instagram Stories with insightful captions to teach users around the world about the plight of animals.

Know it is all about being real when it comes to using Instagram posts to get fans. Do not use questions in any single post, or tell a story that is not true.

3. Go Locally

One of the best ways to build your followers on Instagram is to get to know your neighbors!

Whether you are creating Instagram ads or want to promote your event in a specific area, by going to the search page and clicking on the Places tab, you can see what's happening near you.

To see the geotagged posts for that region, key in the address. Then visit relevant and recent tagged posts-obviously, not those of competing companies-and leave a comment or even an emoji, and follow the person if you like what you see. Hopefully, this will mark the beginning of an organic interaction.

For example, if you are providing life coaching services, you may type in your area accompanied by "entrepreneurs." Local entrepreneurs could be finding a work-time harmony or assisting with personal aspirations or job challenges.

Similarly, if you have a real position where people have signed in on Instagram, click on the pictures of those posters and make sure they are aware of your existence on Instagram, and then visit them.

These are some of the easiest strategies to create the correct way for Instagram fans: no bots, no hacks, just tried and tested methods to reach the viewers and make them supporters!

YouTube for Business

If you promote a product or service then you should simply use YouTube for business purposes. This site receives millions of visitors every day and you might draw some of those tourists back to your website.

Using Etiquette

If you've made a video then you're able to load it to YouTube. You will be required to join what is called tags as part of the loading phase. Those are simply keywords referring to the quality of the film. Good keywords are truly essential when using YouTube for business.

E.g., if your video is about an iPod, and someone typed those words into the search box for YouTube, your video that appears in the search results. Then it might not be so again.

By adding the tags you give people a better chance to find their video. Your tags can be iPod linked so you can have MP3 player tags, MP3 tags, iPod learning, etc. This is the way you could use

YouTube for business because you are giving people more options to locate your content with more tags.

You may expect people to type the term 'iPod' into it, but some people think differently. To you, an iPod is perhaps an MP3 player for someone else. That is the benefit of using YouTube names. When you look for the video material you predict what viewers are going to type in.

When the name is well established you might even use it as a sign. Growing people are likely to use while looking for material on either Google or YouTube, there is no exact statement.

The word Soccer is another good example. That's named in many nations, however, they recognize it as soccer in the USA. While looking for football, somebody can type in soccer so your tags need to show that again.

Categorization of the Content

Even add the correct category to your video so viewers will find it easier. These are pretty important as it's the way YouTube uses filtering through the many videos kept. Millions are there and groups can help speed up queries.

Make sure you've selected the appropriate category for your picture. If you are demonstrating anything then add your video to the group 'how to.' Don't panic if you feel like you want to adjust things and at every moment you are permitted to do so.

I want to add videos to my blog while I am using YouTube for the company. You may have learned of video blogging if you've done some writing. Also recognized as a VLog.

You have the right to name it as VLog after uploading a video to YouTube. It tells YouTube that the playlist in your YouTube channel is a VLog. To get a full grasp of this, you'll need to research things like channels and playlists.

How to get more views on YouTube

The reality of the situation is, if you intend on using YouTube for business marketing, the only way you will boost YouTube views is if you build a beautiful quality video. There are services out there which will get you more views, but you should avoid these things.

You run the risk of having your account banned if you're using underhand viewing tactics and all your videos pulled. Would you like to take that chance? All that hard work that you put into developing your video has been wasted. Just develop custom videos that give value and that people enjoy and you will get more views.

If you offer a service or product and want to reap the benefits of YouTube for business, then create a video to showcase your work. You do not necessarily need to appear on camera. You can develop a slide presentation that contains what you want to say. Just narrate out audibly over the words on display.

Highlight the actual features of the product and of course the benefits. Add photos of the brand name to give even more visual impact. Never get carried away by making it a long-drawn-out production. Keep it simple and keep it short, around two minutes is usually enough.

People love to see visual content and through the creation of a video, you offer good value. Once the slides are finished, simply convert them to a video file and upload them to YouTube. Fill in the video and the YouTube summary box with your email info.

You've produced the video masterpiece of all significance. It's up on YouTube and you're starting to see some views coming to your website and visitors. Now is the moment to ramp up even more of the flow.

You may have learned about Twitter, or maybe not. This is the world's growing social networking platform, which is now Google's second only in terms of resources. Many might say this is much greater. It's just time to learn. The argument I'm trying to say here is that Facebook's huge subscription base is something that you should take advantage of. By letting them work together you can use both YouTube and Facebook for the company.

One thing you can do is promote your video content to your friends on both Facebook and YouTube. On YouTube, you'll notice a sharing icon that helps you to post the video with the Facebook page. Your friends see it and visit your website if they like it. Now when you use YouTube for business purposes, will you start to see the potential?

Using the sharing box on Facebook, you can directly click and post the URL of your YouTube file, as well. It is a rare opportunity to get Videos used for advertisement purposes.

Why not build a Facebook fan page that will spotlight your business or commodity. You should put some YouTube videos that you have made into it. You are already opening things up to Facebook as a whole and the reach is growing.

If you are using YouTube for business purposes, you need to use a bit of imagination to view your content. This opens up a whole new advertisement environment for you.

YouTube Advertising — Will the next Step Take the Brand?

Online video dominates virtually the internet and businesses are striving to keep up with this trend and promote their brand. YouTube is a perfect forum for businesses to make good use of and spread their posts. It is necessary to be mindful that most users visit YouTube for the primary amusement reason and thus companies have to produce and publish YouTube videos that are adequately entertaining.

Many famous brands such as Sony Mobile and Jamie Oliver's Food Tube have adopted video marketing, which takes advantage of YouTube's mammoth audience base to engage with their potential customers. Compared with other conventional methods for leveraging the search engine, videos in your SEO strategy will improve your outreach and draw more clients. Let's consider how YouTube fits into an effective optimization plan for the search engine.

YouTube: Business Success Marketing

Video SEO focused on critical YouTube analytics, will play a significant role in evaluating the effectiveness of your marketing campaign. YouTube is the biggest and strongest video platform on the internet, according to this article quoting Chris Clarke, the chief creative officer at DigitasLBi, the firm that creates YouTube videos for Sony Mobile. Brands are not exploiting creativity from YouTube in the right manner, however. Brands ought to include material that fits with the way YouTube runs and its populations. Only then will they sell YouTube at its potential.

While daunting, the many marketing options available on this popular video channel allow businesses to choose between. It is possible to build pre-roll advertisements that appear before the videos and are skippable. This is an economical option as the advertiser only needs to pay if someone is watching the ad for at least 30 seconds. There's also the option to buy ads that appear at the bottom of the screen during video or purchase on-site display advertising.

Here are a few explanations why you would find ads on YouTube.

- You can upload your video to YouTube absolutely free and easy and share it with others.

- No need to invest in web servers to store your photo, as it can be stored directly via YouTube.

- YouTube quickly speeds up the video's transmission and can reach out to a huge crowd.

Search for the ultimate YouTube App

YouTube has valuable resources that you can use to produce amazing content, distribute videos, develop a large fan base, and promote your brand effectively.

- **YouTube Capture:** This allows you to make movies on the go and capture every moment. You can take as many clips as you want and you can put together any amount of clips. In addition, you can conveniently trim and reorganize the clips from your phone, and even add a soundtrack that you prefer either from your own music library or from the audio library of Capture. Upload the video to YouTube, and add it to all the social networks simultaneously.

- **YouTube Video Editor:** This is another valuable YouTube tool that can be used in your web browser to enhance your uploaded videos. Videos may be mixed, music and text effects are applied, clips trim and rotate, changes introduced, and clips stabilized. Use a control panel you can auto-fix and fine-tune color and lighting, and soothe the video's shakiness. There are options available to change play velocity. You can specify half or quarter velocity, and include smooth effects of slow motion. The tool's blurring facial property detects and eliminates the actors' identity issues. From the approved tracks available in the library, you can also add your favorite music.

- **YouTube Captions:** You can add, modify, or erase captions using this tool, and generate automated captions.

- **YouTube Analytics:** This application allows you to track your videos/channels using state-of-the-art measurements and reports. Information for Views, Traffic sources, and Demographics are available. You can access this tool via YouTube.com/Analytics.

- **Audio Library:** You can download background music for your videos here. It is also absolutely free.

You need to have a clear understanding of the video marketing tactics and trends to gain ultimate success in your business. YouTube is a prominent forum for optimizing your content on screen. Making the most use of the built-in resources provided on the website to boost the visual content and offer the brand full exposure.

Promotion on YouTube

They may also use YouTube to view video images or even entire films. We can create something called 'Infomercials' and load it onto YouTube as well. This can be used as a marketing strategy for the product or service sponsored by YouTube.

But let's first look at how YouTube is in the online world at the moment. Recently YouTube, which Google acquired for $1.65 billion in 2006, has been reported to broadcast 4 billion videos digitally every day. This was seen as an increase of 25 percent in the past eight months in early 2012.

This increase comes at a good time because more and more people watch videos on their smartphones and televisions. Through delivering quality material, Google is promoting the modern form of experience.

YouTube figures indicate that every minute around 60 hours of video is uploaded to the site. That's an amazing figure, unthinkable a few years ago and one you can leverage with the marketing of your goods via YouTube. YouTube broadcasts about 4 billion videos worldwide a day but only about 3 billion of them are reportedly monetized every week.

Checklist Video

It's easy to be skeptical about anything and I understand if you're wondering if the promotion works for YouTube? The reality is that it does, but first, you have to build a video that has excellent content.

You need to have some kind of action plan or a video checklist before you create a video of any sort. Do you know what that material is about your subject? Whether you're planning to chat or narrate so you'll require a form of outline at hand, because you're completely sure that you'll make things up as you move along.

Throughout your YouTube video marketing, one aspect you don't want to happen is to stop because you don't know what to say next or just mumble your way through the whole recording.

Plan what you plan to convey and rehearse until the filming even takes place. Seek to talk with trust and clearness. You want to come off as someone professional about the information you express to the subject.

Shoot some videos of the rehearsals and watch them back. Were you comfortable with the tonality and consistency of your voice? Was there some disturbance in the background? You don't like road noise or, worse still, video driver. If you can get a second opinion before taking the actual film, then do so.

Image Formation

Now it's time to get your video promotion job done on YouTube and get your video camera ready. For true shooting. Does your phone take a good video if you don't have one of these then?

When you want to introduce yourself to audiences you need some sort of video device. Check at all the choices you have and test them out. You will notice that your modest phone would send you the results you need. You will invest in better facilities because you make more sales.

Unless you don't have any sort of video camera for YouTube marketing so what you'd have to do is have pictures of the product inside the video itself. Use PowerPoint or a similar tool to create a slideshow, bring the photos inside, and then narrate your text. Think regarding any advantages and functionality the company has.

Examples of Infomercials can be found on the Web. If you need to know how content should look then search for infomercials on Google quickly. Look for podcasts on video, too.

Add a title to your infomercials and begin with a happy salutation. For your YouTube marketing plan, a strong intro is critical because this is what the audience would initially latch for.

Try finishing the video well, too. Thanks to people for taking the time to watch the video. Attach a call for action and have a connection to your website so people can reach you. Packages like Windows Movie Maker are free and will make some fun video titles and animation.

Of course, the most important part of the video is the actual body. It is where you are going to touch the audience and keep following them. You must make it good otherwise the viewer will be able to click elsewhere.

Try not to sound boring in the video, and keep up to two minutes in length. Engage the listener and still talk in a simple voice. Bu doing this you'll be well on your way to being proud of having a YouTube promotion video.

When anyone enjoys your video they will become a customer. You want users to go back on your page and see if you might sell goods or services.

Be sure you think about what the company will achieve for them, and how it can fix their urgent problems.

Infomercials can be used beautifully for instructional videos too. Why not place them on your site and use YouTube marketing to show what your videos can help people learn. Create a short clip of your tutorial and attach a connection to your web to lure them.

You'll consider making an infomercial that supports you'll be really helpful to someone searching for a career. Mention your talents, your knowledge, and your credentials. All this is basically, are a video resume and you may even mention what kind of work you want. The scope for YouTube advertising here is massive.

Marketing via YouTube

It is time to put it somewhere where people can access it when you are happy with the final video. In my opinion, the best place is YouTube, for two reasons.

Firstly because it gets billions of viewers worldwide every day, it can only benefit you. Imagine how much YouTube traffic you might get as a result of lots of people watching your video. That's a big exposure for your product, service, or business.

Additionally, you ought to hold reducing the rate of YouTube advertising, or as small as possible. And what is the expense of YouTube advertising, you may question yourself? The best thing about YouTube is that you can post a video and host it for free. And the advantage is that you get free YouTube advertising and publicity for your images.

If you plan on adding more than one video to YouTube then setting up your own channel is worthwhile. This will enable you to centralize and brand your videos to yourself. If you want to help with any YouTube promotion, you can customize the look of your channel, although this is not necessary.

Before posting the picture, make sure that the preferred keyword somewhere in it is the name you offer to the video file. When it's posted, apply the keyword to the title and definition. This helps refine the search engine picture, which encourages users to access it. As part of its marketing strategy, your company, whether large or small, requires YouTube promotion. The more viewers viewing your ad, the more often you would be making sales. Today add a video to the content to see if you will profit from it.

Facebook Advertising Activity

It's safe to say that online video has literally exploded in the last couple of years. Digital innovation has driven companies across the world to recognize the promise of a digital content communication approach. YouTube traffic experiences the best video traffic; that is without a doubt.

YouTube has experienced massive growth since its inception. Recent statistics showing that approximately 48 hours of video content is posted to the internet every minute is an indication of the development. I'm sure you will agree this is nothing short of amazing.

There are other video sites around and they are indeed worth uploading your video to. However, the traffic you get from these is nothing compared to what you can expect from YouTube traffic. If people like your product or even your video, then there is a good chance they will come and visit your website to find out more about you.

It does not matter if you want to watch the latest movie trailers, music videos, or just 'how to' videos. Everything you'll find on YouTube.

If you have a business, product, or service, you can benefit from YouTube traffic. Here are some ways to do so.

- **Large Publicity**

  No other video platform will dominate the same kind of viewers worldwide as YouTube. If we need to check out a picture, this is the place we all go to. Now consider how this large base of users will be of use to your company.

- **Create Your Own Canal**

  YouTube lets you build what are called channels. Essentially this is your room to house your photos. You can configure as you wish to screen. If all of the videos are under a channel in one location, it makes them easy to find so, in effect, you'll receive much more YouTube traffic.

As more and more people like the quality of your channel, they would add it to their favorites. You may even get the link linked to your own blog or website.

- **Set Up Your Subscription List**

Perhaps your website includes an opt-in box that gathers names and email addresses. Now you can attach a video to your opt-in box to build a more immersive multimedia look.

I can think of a successful Dating Niche marketer who increased his conversions overnight after embedding video into his opt-in region.

You will use YouTube to host the video and receive a stream of YouTube views and then you will have to link it to the opt-in account.

- **Professional Image**

  Having a video conveys a more professional image on your blog or website. Standard text is perfect but video further improves the website. You can see the video on the website or YouTube, so by getting the video you can seem more credible in some way.

- **Blow Up Traffic**

  YouTube is the largest network that ensures that YouTube traffic flows day and night. Since the planet is split into time zones that means someone in Australia, where it is now morning, might see your video when you're asleep in say London.

  You don't have to post a single photo. Why not create your channel as mentioned above, and add as many videos as you want there. The more you add the better rank you are likely to get on YouTube traffic.

Optimization of Search Engines

YouTube is under Google management. Having two huge websites under one umbrella represents fantastic opportunities for your business.

Google likes video material and would love you much more if you have it on YouTube. Whether it has YouTube video links, the website page should be perfectly tailored for the search engines.

Now Google's search results show both text and video. What if anyone is trying to return your video? Talk of what that would do about your revenue and future YouTube viewers that could be going to your web.

By creating backlinks to your posts, you will increase YouTube traffic. Be sure that you save your files, too.

Audio Samples

If you have published and sent some posts to blog pages then you know how important it can be. People enjoy reading posts and going to the pages of the publication to do exactly that.

It spreads virtually across many sites when an article is syndicated and you get some nice traffic. Imagine that you can do the same for images, and get traffic from YouTube along the way. Well in the form of a video article, now you can.

The most important parts of your text article will be in a video article. You don't need a camera to make this sort of output. What you need are the right tools and a little creativity.

You will turn the text article into a document that the user will interpret in the video on the screen. Instead, you say the words. To spice things up a little, it's worth including certain content such as videos.

A well-made, two-minute video article will give customers tremendous value and bring you some amazing traffic on YouTube.

I created a short production recently about how to combat stress. I've applied text to slides and recorded stuff like meditation too. I also added some music to give more of a professional feel to the production.

The traffic from video posts that you will receive is just as strong as any regular picture. Customers continue to believe you instantly after hearing an individual speech and are delighted to visit your website. You can choose to use traffic statistics from YouTube to track any traffic you get.

As part of whatever YouTube marketing you use in your company, video videos will be doing wonders.

You must be careful to use copyright free music as YouTube has strict guidelines on what you should use. I realize you see a number of several recognized videos on there, but those videos might be deleted in time. All the traffic that you have built up on YouTube is gone in the process. A fast search by Google will take you to certain websites that provide free copyright music to download.

A popular method to use online audio recording is named 'Audacity.' This will allow you to edit the music to match the duration of the video. You can add effects like fading etc. to the music, too. You'll find 'Audacity' by doing a fast internet scan.

When all that goes beyond you then outsource it to someone who can build images, edit music and, so on. We should still be able to post it on YouTube for search engines to refine it.

You get mass exposure for your products by getting more and more YouTube traffic which can only be good in the longer term.

The way you target your marketing campaign will be to provide a video to support your brand. Both subscribers and sales will reap the rewards.

Learn How to Use YouTube Videos to Drive More Traffic to Your Website

YouTube attracts hundreds of millions of users per month who use YouTube to browse for company knowledge and a broad variety of topics. You will find the advantages of using YouTube to advertise your company if you are involved in bringing more traffic to your website and through your monthly income.

YouTube Is one of the most popular online free Marketing Resources

You'll be on the path to strengthening the overall YouTube approach by taking the time to understand how effective Internet marketers are utilizing YouTube to their benefit. You should consider making and uploading promotional videos on YouTube if you aim to bring more traffic to your website or blog to build your company. Business owners, individuals, and professionals uploading videos to YouTube enjoy the advantage of unrestricted traffic without spending any fee.

To Learn Everything You Need to Know about YouTube

Before you start with the high cost of advertising, many internet marketers take the time to learn everything about successful YouTube marketing strategies and video marketing secrets that are being used to market businesses around the world. Signing up for YouTube content preparation is one of the easiest opportunities to discover anything there is to teach. Although there are many books written on the topic, taking a video course on how effectively and efficiently to market on YouTube is the best way to learn everything you need to know about using YouTube to market your business quickly.

Efficient Internet Marketers and Company owners Can benefit by Watching Videos

You should consider watching a YouTube training video or YouTube training videos if you are starting on YouTube first or have been using it for some time, but do not achieve the results you want. Videos from the training are much more effective than books. Another idea you might consider is signing up for a YouTube crash course, training on YouTube, or watching one or more videos from YouTube. In so doing, you'll be on your way to discovering all the information you need to know about YouTube to allow successful use of the web.

Individuals, company owners, and practitioners taking the time to learn from the experts will discover everything they need to know about YouTube promotion and all the other video marketing tricks including, but not limited to, how to gain more impressions on YouTube and how to push YouTube traffic to the website and forums.

YouTube is one of the easiest ways to do ads because of its massive success. To become a good marketer, know the latest YouTube Marketing Tactics.

A Guide to Twitter for Beginners

Twitter is a social network that shares some similarities with certain social networking platforms, such as Facebook.

This can be reached from twitter.com on a device or through the Twitter software on mobile. We may also characterize Twitter as a "micro-blogging" site. Users can compose short "tweets" messages, which are published and shared with the world.

The first thing you'll see when logging in to your Twitter account is your Twitter feed-an ever-updating list of other people's Tweets.

Users

Use Twitter to stay up to date on their favorite celebrities' public affairs, news, and hobbies. This is always being revised and improved, which allows people the impression of being 'on-the-pulse' — breaking news is sometimes reported on Twitter until this happens online.

Think of it as a constant waterfall of information, from which users can decide exactly from whom they want that information. Twitter is also highly interactive-anyone can write a tweet and answer other people's tweets.

If you're acquainted with Facebook (as many people are), certain items would look different on Twitter-you've got a profile picture, you can post updates, you can see other people's activities, and you can connect and communicate with others. There may still be specific aspects so it can take a bit of getting a used to-a couple of these distinctions are mentioned below:

Everything Is available

Unlike Facebook, everything you're posting on Twitter is public and anyone in the world can see it. While your account may be made private, people usually use Twitter to relay their views, viewpoints, and news to the planet. It isn't meant for intimate, one-on-one contact.

You Have no 'Friends'

You may follow any other member on Twitter, without their permission or consent. This doesn't automatically mean you know each other or you're real-life buddies-many users use Facebook to track their favorite celebrities or products.

Simple Tweets

Twitter is not the place for long or updated stories. The tweets are restricted to a maximum length of 140 characters, supporting quick, snappy posts and notifications.

You can simply use Twitter to share a link to content on your website or elsewhere on the web if you have something long to say. Bloggers, bloggers, and news sources can also utilize Twitter to put a fresh report or post to their followers' notice on their website.

Who Makes Use of Twitter?

Twitter has 250 million active users worldwide (according to its corporate website) and around 70% use Twitter on their mobile. While this pales next to Facebook (which continues to have more than 1 billion active users), Twitter users are younger, more varied, and more likely to engage with their favorite products. Twitter is most common among 18-29 year-olds according to this study.

Learning the Lingo

Facebook uses quite a lot of terminology which may seem a bit confusing at first.

On its website, Twitter has an outstanding glossary with a detailed collection of phrases specific to Twitter. We have chosen some of the most important terms below and an explanation for each.

- **Tweet**

  A short message that is released on Twitter (limited to 140 characters) Tweets may include images and text.

- **Hashtags (#)**

  A hashtag (represented by a # symbol) is used to indicate a given topic or discussion trend, such as # Football, # news, or # funny. Click on a hashtag and view a list of tweets containing the same hashtag. If a large number of people use a specific hashtag it is said to be "trending."

- **Follow and Unfollow**

  If you "join" another Twitter account, their tweets will show (see below) in your Twitter Feed.

  You can also pick people to "unfollow."

- **Twitter Feed**

  A selection of messages from people you're following. Your timeline is ordered in sequential order (i.e. newest tweets are at the top) which is continuously refreshed when new tweets are released. This is Twitter's main portion and the first thing you see when you log in.

- ***Twitter Handle***

  The special nickname for Facebook. Grips are followed by a mark @. The BBC, for example, uses the @BBC handle

- **Mentions**

  You simply include their Twitter handle in your Tweet if you want to communicate with another Twitter user. You should be informed then that you listed them. By 'mentioning' each other in your tweets, you can conduct a conversation or discussion with another user (but bear in mind that your conversation is fully open to the public).

- **Reply**

You may respond to a tweet by clicking next to it on the little "reply" icon. Your reaction will begin with the username of certain individuals.

- **RT (Retweet)**

If someone likes your tweet, they'll be able to share it with their own fears. This is also retweeting. Facebook should alert you when you have retweeted one of your messages.

- **Direct Message (DM)**

Although Twitter is public, you can send another user a private message (rather like an e-mail). This is a "direct message" These messages are often restricted to 140 characters, so only anyone who follows you will direct reply.

- **Lists**

  If you follow many people you can organize them into various lists. Those could include things such as friends, celebrities, news, jobs, etc.

Getting Started on Twitter

The best way to get to grips with Twitter is to get your hands dirty and simply dive in. When you've never seen it before, it might sound a bit overwhelming, but fear not! The Twitter website does a good job of holding your hand and telling you what to do next-including selecting a username, finding interesting people to follow, and writing your first tweet.

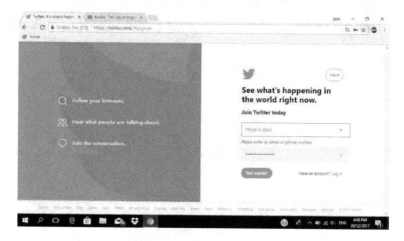

All you need to create an account is an email address. To sign, just go to twitter.com or update your phone or tablet's Twitter software, and follow the directions.

Using Twitter to Run Your Business

Many products and businesses have a Twitter page, so for larger corporations, it is not unusual to hire a professional individual to handle their Twitter account. The BBC, the prime minister, and even the Queen all have an official Twitter presence.

Promote Mode

Are you a budding personal brand or business on Twitter? For $99 per month, automatically promote your Tweets to reach your best audience and grow your followers.

Get started

Learn more

Facebook will acter you an audience of thousands and an ability to connect with your clients in such a manner that conventional methods of advertisement clearly cannot be achieved. Yet it's still a double-edged knife and can go horribly times.

You Can't Be a Cheerleader

You can't go in as a company and just blot out promotional ads as you can on television or in magazines. You need to be prepared for a possible reaction of criticism, cynical comebacks, and mockery-particularly if you're running a major company, or often controversial. And in conventional ads, you're not in complete charge on Twitter-you're exchanging the leverage with your viewers. It may be scary, but it can be employed to great advantage if you get it correctly.

Take a glance at the Innocent Drinks Twitter page as a perfect illustration of a business that respects and is able to create with its customers.

Managing your Twitter page with your business can be enjoyable, and if handled properly it will potentially allow you to boost revenue. When you are reasonably comfortable that you can devote enough energy to it, then get in there and do it!

The Impact of Ads on Twitter

Digital technology has made our lives so comfortable and successful that we consider ourselves almost unable to survive without it today!

The marketing landscape is already being affected by the growing internet channels used to easily target customers around the globe.

Any of these online platforms were not initially meant for advertisement but found a place in that field recently.

- Entrepreneurs have developed resources they've never thought of getting at their disposal.

- Facebook is one of the devices that was not meant for advertisement but was just a social network.

- Twitter is a large community of connected and interrelated individuals already knowledgeable about the internet.

This is the ideal combination to promote your company, your brand, or whatever products and services you are expected to offer.

Start by becoming a Twitter account and you're off to win over the Twitter community!

Firstly, you should develop a marketing plan complete with your company's strategies and goals.

You will provide descriptions of how you are going to show your business and what deals you are providing.

Effective strategies that present the industry in a good way with a discreet strategy should be employed.

If you're too aggressive, you'll be creating negativity and the results won't be what you planned or wanted.

Provide valid explanations for the consumer to buy the goods and provide some testimonials where appropriate.

A good marketing strategy would help you start started on the right foot and enjoy the benefits of improved revenue and earnings.

It's important to get the whole picture of your business status as you create marketing strategies that enable you to achieve your goals.

Twitter offers many useful tools to help you track the traffic on your website, your followers, their tweets, and additional information to help you plan your advertising campaign more effectively.

You will know quickly how your company is valued, what your supporters think of your business, and how happy your customers are.

You can change and adapt your strategies with this plethora of details.

Twitter's other powerful advantage is that you can communicate directly with your customers.

This is critical in business because it provides a more intimate connection with certain customers.

Customers who are happy and satisfied will spread the word and give you the best and most affordable word-of-mouth advertisement known to man.

Regardless of their busy schedules and strict timelines, consumers tend to shop digitally and if they can find your company on Facebook, they can have your company at their fingertips; this is where you tend them!

Your traffic will increase through leaps and boundaries, and profits will increase exponentially. The mission is underway and you should constantly be refining and executing it. Once you have your plan that's complete with strategies and goals, you're going to want to start considering the audience you want to attract and how you're going to achieve that. Effective strategies should be applying and following the solid strategy you have in place.

Getting your picture on your Twitter page is even more successful.

This will offer the company the personal touch and not sound that the customers are talking to an organization or an anonymous individual.

Create your Twitter profile carefully, too; consumers can read this and see who you are and what your company is about. Hold it simple, succinct, and descriptive.

Your Twitter account will operate more efficiently for you by utilizing a few other communications instruments.

Use Hootsuite.com and Tweetdeck.com to update schedules and post your social media messages simultaneously over social media browsers like Facebook, Twitter, and LinkedIn.

Hootsuite lets you plan tweets at no expense in advance. It may be hard for you to have a presence on Twitter for some days, so this tool allows you to schedule a tweet whenever you want to share an idea or find a link you want to talk about.

Such apps can also help you manage your Twitter page and activities more efficiently, and will help you submit messages while you're focused on any other part of your company.

To be competitive in the internet business, you need to keep as educated and up-to-date as possible.

You must keep up with the latest news, fads, and trends that sometimes happen very quickly.

Your core marketing strategy with Twitter needs to be about customer interaction.

As part of the promotional strategy, a customer on Twitter wants to share his thoughts and suggestions. Twitter promotes this contact and this engagement should gain the trust of the consumers.

This is one of the most important pillars of use messaging on Twitter:

- You can use Twitter as an effective marketing tool for your company by going through some simple steps.

- Follow people of like minds who are already interested in your product.

- Millions of Twitter users are added every day and many of them have a problem that can solve your product.

- Connecting with those people who would be interested in what you have to offer, is of utmost importance. Many customers continue to follow a person back from whom they have obtained an invitation to join; you will cash in on this client group who is looking for your company.

- Note that Twitter is a networking network site; the reason for engagement is fascinating dialogue.

- You don't want to appear desperate; involve consumers in meaningful discussions on what you've got to sell.

- Don't be too blunt with a sales message that you are pushing them further.

If you want to sell goods to somebody you don't know as well, you will be courteous, respectful, and cautious. Initially, developing a conversational partnership would work way better than confronting followers with a high-pressure sales pitch which instantly loses them. The digital market is somewhat close to the conventional industry: nothing wants a seller with heavy energy! Take your time, and build lifelong consumers who inform their friends about your company and share a strong positive word.

You might not be able to use the stereotypical handshake but it would be almost as important to get a strong solid statement on the company.

Tweet your followers regularly. An adage that is quite descriptive of Twitter is out of sight, out of view.

Tweets have a limited existence so the consumers don't see you because you're not posting.

When you tweet regularly, your clients will recognize that your company is alive and healthy and that you can deliver the same goods and services at the same price. Tweet at least once a day; data reveals that fewer than 10 percent of Twitter followers check to see what was posted yesterday.

When you aren't consistently there, you'll lose their interest. Have a constant Twitter icon.

Viral media campaign edition of Twitter is Retweeting!

When retweets scatter around Twitter, you can bring enormous value and encourage ongoing conversations. For retweets, you'll even draw thousands of potential customers; your viral media strategy would be up and running.

This tidal wave of awareness and publicity can be a disruptive factor in market and profit development for your company. One of the most powerful ways to receive more retweets is to write tweets about things like "how to."

Everyone loves learning how to do projects and you will build a broad retweeting program by sharing this sort of detail.

People are attempting to do-it-yourself ventures in this downturned environment so you will provide the skills that they need to achieve their job cost-effectively and promptly.

Be sure to provide links to the website and can include more material regarding the subject and any associated product you sell.

It would increase your earnings because you spread your learned expertise.

Research shows that performing Twitter polls where you give the participants some excellent incentives would drive traffic and company into your Twitter page. Everyone likes something easy, and you can attract large numbers of followers and their followers to increase your future client base.

This is an easy concept that will work to draw up a chart for you to use on your marketing plans in certain promotions.

Another tactic you need to adopt is to connect all your social networking sites to Twitter.

For both of these media networks followed by the consumer base, the ad strategy would be more robust and successful in its method.

You will leave no stone unturned in cyberspace.

With the amount of everyday usage combined with a continuous link of smartphones on such social networking platforms, the promotional dollars could yield benefits that you never thought could have been feasible.

In many countries around the world, the company will be open 24/7; the sun will never fall on your thriving business.

Don't redesign the chair.

You will extend your Twitter awareness by reading other people's success stories while you study Twitter's marketing possibilities.

Learn various tips that benefited them when they began, and what worked for them.

If it weren't successful with them, take it off the plan to do and pass on to the next approach.

Using those who have come before you as best practices make your path easier and save you valuable time and money.

Bring traditional marketing into your campaign on Twitter.

You will need to remind any client you have of having a Twitter account now.

They can find useful information here, as well as any deals that you bring to your clients.

Place the Twitter connect and other traditional marketing resources on all business cards.

This is a method of keeping the customer updated on patterns, goods, and other useful information in real-time.

If you are using technologies they are acquainted with to promote your business, the consumer may consider your business as cutting edge.

Participate in Twitter Conversations until you get acquainted with Twitter.

There are frequently scheduled meetings, which are set up by a moderator. Every chat has a subject that the participants are involved in.

A featured guest may also tend to address questions and respond to followers on a technical basis. At the end of the session, a helpful Chat transcript will be given. Twitter chats can offer you the ideal opportunity to create new relations with people of similar interests as you.

You will recognize and link potential clients as an expert on the topic; this will create faith and trust in you and the product that you are giving them.

Followers can appreciate you more, and broaden your list of followers that can create more sales. That certainly creates competence in this field that you have.

Followers engaged in these daily talks are now deeply interested in the niche in question. They can be a wealth of knowledge and provide the company with external ties, tips, and tools.

This will provide the future buyer with a way to see a virtual face behind a company that can improve leads and contacts.

Following along is one of the best chances you'll get on Twitter.

You want users to follow you, but from those users, you follow you can gather several customers. If you're not following anyone back, you should give the message that you're on Twitter for sales and promotions only.

This is an egotistical argument that won't yield good results; you won't create trust with one-sided followers.

Leading along is a potential indication of concern and attention not to be ignored in the communication campaign.

Using Twitter's @mentions tool to help you create deeper connections and attract the interest of a more focused audience.

This method guides the tweet to a single person and acts as something of a one-on-one approach.

Your aim isn't to instantly offer them a product; it's a call to action that involves them without the urgency involved with a sales pitch.

You build a partnership that can cause a transaction after the partnership has been formed.

Such relationships should evolve with time and maturity and they will be more apt to react, retweet, and communicate with you.

True business prospects arise from actual relationships; this is an important resource to bear in mind as you set up your marketing strategy on Twitter

You want to move these visitors to your advertising or industry page, after contacting your followers on Twitter. When your users develop more confidence and trust in you, they'll start exploring who you are in the marketplace and what your company can do for them.

Upload tempting ads with condensed URLs that guide them to your website.

If the knowledge you give is important and meaningful to them, they will look deeper into your company.

Tweet swaps are another aspect of Twitter that you can use as a weapon in your marketing toolbox.

That is analogous to ad swaps in which you advertise on the list of another party and they advertise on your list. Your Twitter fans are on your list to hear more about you, read your posts, and keep up-to-date with new developments in the niche they love.

You're not going to be generating money from tweet swaps; you're just going to be creating concepts and moving traffic.

This can increase your reach, which will help you create a committed, long-term follow-up that can make money for you. You will reach the followers of another through tweet exchanges, and catch them through your thoughts and offers.

Find a friend on Twitter that has a niche close to yours.

You will have similar communication tactics but not exactly the same ones.

Don't only search for anyone with a large number of followers; you want consistency over volume or the followers won't be of much value to you. The better approach is to give these fans a free product, instead of automatically attempting to sell them a product. This method is for lead generation and not a sales promotion.

One of the most fascinating ways to create a detailed follow-up on Twitter is to post questions about any subject, but ideally, one on which you have a wealth of information.

In your conversations with your fans, you will have responses to certain concerns. This establishes you as a subject expert and helps create confidence and continuity between you and your fans.

Starting a conversation on a fun yet difficult subject with others can create a group of followers who listen to your tweets and reply with their own helpful thoughts and ideas.

This is a discreet way to advertise the company utilizing the knowledge you carefully gathered. Awareness is a strength and you want to be able to do Twitter marketing for you.

Although there is no right or wrong way to use Twitter in your marketing plan when you communicate with your fans you can adhere to the unwritten rules that guarantee you successful exposure and great reviews.

Proper Twitter etiquette will go a long way toward establishing total relationships that will boost sales and profit.

Create a schedule that involves how much time you spend working on your Twitter page.

Many times it's possible to lose track of time and end up finishing a conversation that you began with your followers in the wee hours of the morning.

Place enough time to post your content on Twitter, and contact your fans.

Keep as close to your regular period as you can, and make the best of every contact you partake in.

The 80-20 law exists in promotions both in Twitter ads and in conventional advertising ways. When you are always bragging about yourself or selling your company, nobody would want to speak to you about the topics.

You should add tweets regarding subjects directly relevant to your career, include valuable knowledge that will enhance other people's lives, and informative conversations that cover a range of things.

Give numerous tweets when engaging with your followers; don't over-promote yourself or company.

As in most partnerships, a corporate partnership is a two-way path.

You have to demonstrate an interest in your customer before they purchase a product from you to win their faith and confidence.

Cross support the brand campaigns through the Twitter handle that you have. Use every resource at your fingertips on the network and combine these to function smoothly and efficiently for you.

Connect your email and URLs for any tweet you create so a follower can quickly reach you outside the Twitter network.

See the content of the messages very closely.

If you use your Twitter page as a publicity tool, you want the public to see what you are referring to.

You have no idea where these messages are going to be exchanged and you avoid negative or intense conversations.

Don't mention something you don't do in person on your Twitter page.

Avoid being too close or acquainted with the clients and no conflicting signals can be interpreted.

Still stay polite, honest, and respectful of your words. Innuendos and off-color remarks are not appropriate.

Placed other people's needs above your desires.

Not all of you and your Twitter media account; it's a chance to create a positive partnership that can carry sales and benefits to the organization in the future. Take the time to listen to others, appreciate them and their opinions, exchange material, and not impose the viewpoints and thoughts on them. Be involved, and be polite.

Using business language or terms that people do not learn or appreciate is one of the rudest things you may do with your messages.

You don't want to look rude while engaging with your audience.

Don't use industry-specific rhetoric; it could annoy the viewer.

You've got a brief period to catch their imagination and attention; don't use terms to look up or challenge you to describe them.

You don't want to act as a corporate robot whose aim is to sell a product and pass on to the next client.

Consider behaving positively when communicating with future clients.

Do not be condescending or patronizing towards them; they will not respond positively to you and will shift towards a more user-friendly person to work with.

Twitter one of today's most important communication resources is.

It is a real-time source of current trends, knowledge, and engagement that can easily catch and push a viewer to buy the product that you are selling to them. You can tap into the power of Twitter marketing right away with a solid plan and implementation process for your product. As you plan your marketing strategy, include this cutting edge technology that is exploding in the marketplace today!

How Your Business Can Build Up more Twitter Followers

It's unusual to talk to a company owner using Facebook while not having more fans. Others may claim the statistics aren't relevant because they're all for "price followers," but it's usually the ones that just have a few followers that make the statement.

What would you want more Twitter followers as a business owner? Three good reasons for this:

1. More followers have power in civil affairs. The higher your follower counts, the more people (your customers) assume you are an expert or at least somebody interesting and

popular. It may not be valid but it's how it works in a world where everything has a ranked list.

2. Your power spreads to more fans. Twitter is the best platform to bring concepts out to a wider audience. If you have ideas worth sharing, why wouldn't you have them spread to as many people as you can? Twitter makes doing that ridiculously easy. The larger the supporters count, the quicker they distribute and share their ideas.

3. More fans contribute to greater revenue. For one of three factors, you're usually on Twitter: being amused, networking with others, or selling your things. If it's a company, a commodity, a service, or even a cause, more followers are generating more leads and more clicks. It is a perfect publicity resource for small businesses.

Until I share any tips about how to increase the number of your followers on Twitter, I guess I must advise you on how not to do it first.

Try not to cheat the system, and try to attract thousands of followers overnight instantly. When it looks too amazing to be real then it is definitely. If you're a star who has built up a massive following on every other social outlet, it may require time and energy to attract fans so the commitment would be worth it.

What does it mean to buy followers? After all, there are lots of citizens who support this form of operation.

The first excuse you'd not like to do it is that it goes against the laws of Facebook. But the reality that these so-called followers have completely no affiliation, relation, or involvement in you or your company, is worse than that. That will be like giving the business a direct mail to a general, un-targeted list. It will be useless to mention it.

Instead of following these seemingly fast-track methods to build up your count of followers, I want to share some of my favorites tested ways of having more loyal Twitter followers with you.

- **Engage and Know**

  Twitter is mostly about dedication. It's a big, fast-moving site, and you need to produce content that can teach, inform, entertain, or encourage your fans. It can be achieved by exchanging a healthy mix of information, with your people as well as others. Eventually, you can create a huge audience of people who want to hang out with you and join you because they enjoy what you say or post.

- **Keep Attached to Tour Twitter Click**

  When you want your website users to follow you on Twitter then make sure they see a connection to your Twitter icon. They ought to make it clear. Should not hide the Twitter icon at the bottom of your article or web tab. Let it shine and invite tourists to join you. They are interested in hearing more about you and what you have to suggest because they are on your page.

- **Set "Join Me on Facebook" in Your Signature Post**

  Have a connection to your Twitter account in your E-mail signature. (An email signature is a tiny piece of information that is immediately added to the end of an email address. People usually add their name and contact details in the email signature; but, you're free to write whatever you like.) Make it simple to follow you on Twitter. Do not have them look for you ever again.

- **Add your Twitter ID to the Letterheads and Business Cards**

  Although this won't create you a big follow-up very fast it's a nice practice to get in and it's just as necessary to include your physical location, phone number, and email address.

- **Stop Over-promoting**

  Yeah, please be cautious when sharing your blog entries, goods, etc. on Facebook. There is an unseen barrier you're not supposed to touch. Whether you did, either you're feeling like a spammer or simply ignorant. Not only are you not going to get new fans, but you are also going to wear out your existing followers and many of them are just going to follow you.

- **Follow other People active on Twitter**

  Begin your networking activities by being a follower of the individuals in your business you respect. Read their messages to get a picture of who they are on Instagram, and what their ambitions are. It's a smart idea to monitor as many people as possible in your business or field. Once you've found people and started to follow them, they'll have the chance to see both your good content and your activity online. Instead, they are more inclined to reciprocate and join you up, as are all of their friends, who may also turn out to be future customers.

- **Place Your Name on Twitter into Mainstream Media Promotions**

Whether you're advertising ads in newspapers, on TV, or radio, you have to make sure your Twitter identity is available for all to see and hear. Only apply the # (hashtag symbol) preceded by the name or logo of the business and you will be noticed by people.

- **Make the Comments Brief enough for You to Retweet**

Retweets are the only way people who don't follow you will get heard, so you have to make the articles convenient for someone to retweet. And keep your tweets brief enough to encourage users to add the RT icon and username ("RT @yourcompanyname.") So, let's assume, for example, if your name is 14 characters long and you would also need to have the room. This ensures the message should be no longer than 126 characters (140-14=126) if it is to be retweetable.

- **Get Your Facebook Twitter Connection**

Quick everybody uses Facebook, and when they enter your Facebook page, it's simple for them to move over to your Twitter account. The ideal place would be in the segment "Around."

- **Tweet Regularly**

  View Twitter as a stream that runs continuously. Tweets run by and are never seen again. So you need to keep your Messages going so you don't get missed. Be transparent. Stand out in the crowd and you'll be attracting even more fans.

- **Link to Twitter to LinkedIn**

  It's great to have a Twitter connection on your LinkedIn page. You are required to use three connections on the LinkedIn profile, so make sure your Twitter page is one of those. It will be perfect for networking especially with your industry's movers and shakers.

- **Publicly Addressing some**

  I used to react to people via Direct Message, assuming that what I had to suggest was meaningless to most followers of mine. Since I didn't respond in public this rendered me appear sociable. Right now, I'm responding almost entirely in secret, because actually, the only people who see such messages are those that follow me and the guy I'm responding who's only a tiny subset of my followers. My messages are sociable but not distracting in any way.

- **Be good at referring to others, and retweeting them**

Facebook encourages social philosophy. The more you connect to someone, the more users you are going to reciprocate, and that's just what needs to happen to increase your count of followers. You require someone to introduce yourself to their supporters. Don't press for too standard a retweet though. It's okay once in a while because if you only post material worth retweeting, people would gladly do it for you without having to ask!

These tips do help raise the numbers of followers and we trust they can send you some motivation. That said, you need to remember: if you're at the beginning of your Twitter trip, there's just nobody going to give you a lot of attention.

Initially, your tweets may be lost in a sea of other updates vying for publicity, but on the other side there won't be that many people reading your updates before you build up a major following, and now is the best opportunity to make a lot of errors.

Note: Twitter requires a lot of effort, has a steep slope in learning, and can be a fairly frightening place to be for the first day. There are all those confusing characters and symbols, odd shortened links, the pressure to follow people you don't know and so many daunting acronyms and buzz words, not to mention the hashtag.

Even if you have a lot to know and have to put in some work, you'll always have a lot of fun and it will certainly improve your company and your name.

Chapter 3

Reasons Why You Aren't Using Social Media Correctly

So far there are 500 million people on Facebook. 64 percent of Facebook users search each day on their Facebook account.

Twitter users number 645,750,000, and 58 million messages are written every day. 2.1 billion returned search queries will be led to Twitter within one day of browsing the internet.

It is estimated that there will be over 5 billion Internet users in 2020, and over half of all users worldwide will have access to the Internet through handheld tablet devices and 80 billion wired devices.

So what do those numbers mean for your company?

In short, this implies that potentially your company should be active on social media. It is a perfect tool for a business owner to quickly and personally create awareness. But only if you do it well.

The issue with this kind of advertisement is that most company owners don't know how to successfully manage this level of exposure and potential.

1. If You're Not Socially linking to Profits, otherwise Your Company Will Be harmed

    The issue is that most people don't go on Facebook or Twitter specifically trying to purchase a good or service. An organization wants to use social networking to bring prospective buyers to its website and create brand awareness in the social world.

There are transformations where the shopping cart is: The account. Varying the posts styles on your pages will help turn the "likes" into sales.

Creating brand awareness is an ample incentive to create your social profiles. Your social networks are a way for clients to get to know the true "you" in a very visible and open environment

2. Not Monitoring Your Data on Your Page

When you don't have a way to monitor where the website traffic is coming from, your online presence attempts are lost. How will you know that if you don't control statistics, your Facebook contest would produce a strong conversion?

Using free monitoring tools such as Google Analytics will help you calculate items like transactions that are helped so you can see how society functions in the revenue process.

3. Not Monitoring the correct Data

And you're scoffing at #2 because you've enabled Google Analytics and you're testing your Facebook data. But can you control things, right? There are tons of indicators tied to social networking, but they're not always explicitly linked to the bottom line.

The amount of 'likes' on a Facebook profile, for example, isn't a perfect measure of how effective the campaign is. What is a "list" if you don't have some commitments? The easiest way to monitor the social network is anything like 'engagement score' (people on a page thinking about us/the number of likes). The commitment rate is a perfect metric to equate with website traffic from various channels. Will your involvement contribute to future consumers reading material on your website?

4. Not Cross-Promoting Sites for Social Networking

Marketing on social media is not on a platform-to-platform basis. The best approach to get the most visibility is to use every network together. Let's presume you are a restaurant with fifty 5-star ratings reported on Yelp. Don't let Yelp be the only forum to make the success stand out. Upload, and talk about, your Yelp reviews on your Facebook account.

Another suggestion is to post the posts on your different sites.

Essentially, try whatever you can to build the maximum favorable publicity imaginable for yourself. Social media marketing can help your company tremendously or it can be a total waste of your time with the amount of exposure and interaction on social media platforms.

Make sure you are using the channels correctly and to their maximum capacity otherwise, you won't see what impact social media can have on your company. If you just continue, there is going to be some trial and error. A post is about to fall flat, a customer complains. The value you can get from social media however far outweighs any challenges and commitment along the way.

Where Social Media in 2020 Is Going

Trends to watch on social media:

- A marketing strategy for social media is in the minds of many small business owners. And if you don't have it on yours it will be!

- Big websites such as Facebook, Twitter, LinkedIn, and, Instagram is competing for market shares by changing their operating strategies to align delivering decent returns to customers with improving customer experience.

- As these channels grow, the way you use them for your small company often needs to shift.

- Let's look forward to certain means of supporting the social networking sector by 2020.

Via Facebook

More than 18 months later the Federal Trade Commission formally found that Facebook consumers were misled by Cambridge Analytica. Without permission from users, the corporation has collected the personal details from millions of Facebook accounts and then used them for political advertisement purposes.

Although Cambridge Analytica went bankrupt soon after the debacle, Facebook is still working hard to improve the processes of data exposure and to convince people to trust the new dedicated news platform.

Google carried Google News out to a group of people in the United States. That means Facebook News can publish material from a team of journalists (employed by Facebook) while you'll still see updates from family and friends on your main page.

The business is also focused on crypto-currency this year and set up its Facebook Pay app. This may mean your small company will quickly be able to add selling on-platform into your budget.

Although the launch of Facebook Watch didn't go as planned (only 140 million users watch the videos and shows every day, which sounds big, but isn't relative to the 1.6 billion regular interaction overall on the platform). Even, it seems like in 2020 Facebook will make another attempt, and let's see what it means for video marketing.

What do those improvements refer to in the communication plan for social media?

We are going to have to watch and see. The more proprietary content the firm produces, the more advertisers can fight to remain noticeable.

Recently, the company announced that it would stop running political ads and is reviewing its global privacy policy to provide consumers with more detail about what data marketers might get.

We're still curious about what the vice president of design and research at the organization, Dantley Davis, intended by his recent announcement about a series of changes that could be heading to the app as early as next year.

How will that affect how you promote your social media business?

You may have the option to restrict who can retweet your tweet (which I can't imagine is a function businessmen will use a ton, we enjoy our retweets!), and the opportunity to tweet things based on their preferences to a different audience.

Learn all about how to use the hashtags on Twitter.

LinkedIn has been the world's biggest technical networking site since its introduction in 2003.

Microsoft purchased the network in 2016 for $26.2 billion, so we've had improved technical expertise and more personalized advertising through exposure to Microsoft's tools.

We saw LinkedIn groups make a comeback too.

A LinkedIn community helps your company to create a board for conversation relevant to your industry. This offers you the chance to create a mutual interest community of like-minded individuals which is unique to your company, service, and/or skills.

Groups can provide excellent exposure for your company, as every participant who is part of your community can feature your logo in their profile. Community members also now have the option to upload different media forms such as photos and videos, and instant updates provide for real-time conversations.

Executive Suite has more than 300,000 participants and puts together leaders with a web series, practical advice, and forums for conversation.

What do you mean by LinkedIn Groups for your small business?

Hopefully, a great means of promoting a sense of belonging, seeking applicants for available roles, and increasing brand recognition to name a couple.

Instagram Headlines

Instagram investigating the elimination of likes in many nations, including Australia, Japan, Italy, and Ireland, you can remember. Likes aren't gone-in the US and Canada you can always show the like count on your own images and videos-just not content from anyone.

So whence came this? The Facebook-owned Instagram has long struggled with users utilizing shortcuts and workarounds. These mostly come from bots and unscrupulous companies who exploit the app to make themselves or other consumers look more famous than they really are. So, it's a bid to make Instagram more real.

Instagram said, "We hope this check can eliminate the burden on how many people a post wants to get, and you can concentrate on sharing the stuff you enjoy."

Though this is perfect for many startups and small companies, influencers and video marketing firms aren't.

When does it inform businesses when famous they are? Why will they demonstrate commitment?

But that might be a positive thing for the typical small business owner who doesn't purchase likes or manipulate the machine with bots.

When the communication plan for social networking involves entertaining posts and you're able to rely on feedback and expanded fans, otherwise you're going to be great.

Although IGTV started off to a late start, it is now deemed one of the best phenomena in social media out there. When Instagram revealed earlier this year that Instagram would require a one-minute overview of IGTV videos on the mainstream for Instagram, users (and businesses) started to take note.

Unlike your other Instagram images, IGTV images can last for 10-60 minutes. This provides a perfect platform for video marketers to conduct interviews, videos behind the scenes, and a lot more.

Since we can now also add landscape-oriented videos, I added my Business Edge Show videos that got lots of traction.

These are just a few of the changes you can expect to see across this year's major platforms. When the year goes by, I'm sure there will be even more, because things are still evolving!

In order to market the company successfully on social media for 2020, it is important not only to recognize but also accept, social networking patterns.

When you feel that keeping on top of social networking is a struggle, consider recruiting an agency who will design plans that are unique to your social media needs and priorities so you can concentrate on developing your company.

Build the Most successful Advertising Strategy for Social Media

There's a vast sea of information out there on social media. There are experts everywhere and there are only so many opinions about best practices and tactics.

Not just this, but the apps themselves are continually evolving, whether it introduces additional functionality, raises character limits, or updates laws elsewhere.

That's why I developed this guide to help you understand how to set the goals for 2020 in social media. This post is especially relevant for you because you have never taken stock of your marketing strategies or generated targets.

It's very essential that you be frank about your achievements and shortcomings in this phase. It's all right to say that some of what you've achieved was a waste of effort that's why we are here.

Here's my three-step plan for determining the 2020 social network targets:

1. Check the Files

    Holding records is a must because you want to better evaluate the effectiveness and productivity of what you spend time posting online. There are several ways to customize a survey, but if you need guidance and motivation, Smartsheet has a free social networking analysis prototype to get you going.

    You need to continue to see beyond the number of views to realize how the content is actually doing. Will people like it, post it, and send remarks about it?

    Pay careful attention to indicators such as engagement-this useful knowledge is how the ability drives someone to tell you what they loved or didn't like. But keep this in mind while preparing the material for 2020.

    I am making an attempt, for example, to post useful information on our Twitter page every day.

    Each site provides free insights on the results of the profile from Twitter to Facebook so use it!

This online coverage lets you see what's gone good and what's fallen flat. Search for the subjects that have been of frequent concern to guests and fans, and post some of the material in the future.

When you are up to the task you might do any paying market marketing. You can still contact us and let us do the heavy lifting so that you can focus on running your firm.

We're always on Facebook, Twitter, LinkedIn, YouTube, and Instagram. Yet, we keep on top of the new developments yet ideas, and love to review surveys and figures!

2. Test Analytics

Sure, you want to look ahead but you do need to look back. You can post material left and right but it does not fulfill its function unless it is directing people to your website. You want to bring customers to the web, where they are likely going to connect more and purchase you a good or service.

Google Analytics is Google's free platform and is essential to preparing the social network for 2020. It tells you how the acts of the company on social drive traffic are broken down into loads of related stats.

Navigate to the Social Acquisitions segment to see these findings and then press Network Referrals. You may use the corresponding year as the date set. You will also be able to see how many users clicked on your links and then landed on your website.

Read Marketing Tips on Social Media for 2020

Will Social networking ads no longer work for you?

Should you know whether you can change to get better results?

I am offering 5 helpful tips in our Tea Time Tip: Advertising for Busy Entrepreneurs and you can know what is, what isn't and what you need to think about further. Read more on our website.

3. Place the goals

The first two phases will offer you a sense of where you are and now is the time to build your strategy. You have a better understanding of what kind of marketing has succeeded, what channel your target market is hanging out on, and where you can concentrate your efforts in the coming year.

You need to do other stuff to achieve your goals:

Track the development of your followers month by month. When you're not attracting new fans all year long, you ought to think about why this is so.

Hold an eye on which seasons the content at a specific site is most common. Pinterest rates, for example, indicate elevated use throughout the summer and at Christmas, with major falls in spring and fall.

Only content that has value to share. You want to sell without having to drive people away. You do want to offer non-sales people tools such as forums, motivational quotations, events — whatever makes sense to the company and audience.

I post posts, events, and news on the LinkedIn page at our service, for example.

The greatest error you might make is to make your marketing strategies a burden, not a productive part of your success. If you enjoy yourself, you can notice that you post material that is more entertaining and collaborative.

If setting the goals for overcoming social media in 2020, keep in mind that you may not always meet them. That is not an error! So long as you're armed with a good communication strategy for social media and what you're posting is genuine and truthful, then you're doing fantastic work!

Chapter 4

Influencer Marketing Is Now Bigger Than Digital Ads

People are online looking at their phones everywhere you look and interact with various social platforms.

If you haven't heard, we're surrounded by all four sides of influencer marketing.

We constantly inhale and exhale marketing influencers every day and yet many of us are not fully aware of what it really is.

While the world is modernizing and the voice of the people is growing, we have broken into a new era of digital marketing, a more natural kind of marketing carried out through influencers.

Influencer content may be framed as testimonial advertising where they themselves play the role of a potential buyer or are third parties.

It identifies the individuals influencing potential buyers and orients marketing activities around them.

"Influencer marketing is turning influencers into company advocates."

Before we go into any details concerning this type of marketing, one should know clearly what it is.

What's Influencer Marketing?

This kind of marketing focuses on promoting the brand's message to a customer, rather than big groups of consumers.

Here, the individual is referred to as the 'influencer' hired to get the word out for your brand.

Those influencers may be the potential buyers themselves in this influencer marketing game.

In general, they play the roles of content writers, journalists, bloggers, CEOs, creative people, marketers, or advisors.

They are connected to other people around them and seek advice and opinions and are considered to be influential.

Content marketing and social media marketing are seen as the two main influencer marketing forms.

How Does Marketing Work?

Nowadays, consumers offer more reactions to scores on a person's social media or thoughts than to believe in advertisements.

This has also the foundation of influencer marketing, where an influencer in their personal and media networks blogs on the goods.

People prefer to trust on the internet, what the influencers have to tell about it.

Most research agencies don't even have marketing power on their radar because it is just a special product form. In certain instances, it is out of their reach because it takes over more of a human voice than the traditional generic corporate ad.

The customers don't send digital advertising the same immersive and emotional reaction.

The reviews and ratings on social media for a specific company or commodity often contribute significantly to the product or service being advertised, which becomes the latest medium for product promotion.

How is brand influencer larger today than physical advertising? & how could they achieve that?

Confidence and integrity are key marketing elements.

We all recognize which media we trust and mistrust and in most situations clearly by the header of the topic.

Traditional media are being scrambled with misinformation and the general consumer would rather interact on a social level with their products or services of interest.

Consumers do not purchase products or services until they are absolutely satisfied that the commodity or service is in all ways suitable for their needs.

When you control the subconscious, it's known that you have the universe in your possession and that's what influencers do.

Influencers have set established partnerships to build trust to become influencers. There's been a lot of dedication and caring to develop such links.

When it comes to establishing partnerships and generating a meaningful image for a particular brand that requires a higher expectation for influencer marketing relative to traditional ads.

Let's turn the light on, Marketing influencer as 'The next big thing.'

"Virtual networking," as seen on.

When the environment shifts to social media, customers turn to fellow users to tell their purchasing decisions.

Instead of looking at companies, as they have done in the past, they are now looking at each other and their favorite personalities, who are consolidating massive results on YouTube, Instagram, Snapchat, Pinterest, LinkedIn, Twitter, Facebook, Google+ and other platforms.

The emergence of the influencer in social media has generated a landscape of potential;

This also created a stream of modern waterworks for marketers to specifically and on a broader scale interact with customers by more authentic, traditional communication forms of leverage like a new era word of mouth.

It provides a clearer definition of a website for Online Messaging. Through social networking contact or response, it facilitates the likelihood of hundreds of more users seeing the post via their network's mutual connections.

Although digital advertisements consist primarily of accurate facts about the items, an influencer strategy to the market has its own methods of enticing consumers in a more engaging, marketing environment with all the accurate definition and knowledge about the products and services that have an organic presence to the advertisement.

Influencers are confident that they will provide the updated details of the products or services they are dealing with, and the message can also be released slowly over many weeks or months.

It's called an influencer's task to gather all the information on the ad strategy and send the word on to customers.

The influencers also get compensated for their jobs to ensure this. If not compensated, then the organization with whom they operate, or in certain situations exchanging material with their readership, provides them with opportunities with no other purpose than informing and promoting network engagement.

Most of the time, unlike digital ads, influencers are "not offering something" and are simply sharing information to create a more positive influence network or to promote participation and interaction on issues that can really benefit. They might choose to follow up with other communication methods such as an email newsletter to promote advertising services or products.

Consumers could soon move away from the old and obsolete knowledge.

Citizens are more inclined to believe people than advertising

Influencer marketing has the idea of 'name of mouth.' Influencer marketing has the definition of 'terms of mouth.' Where ads may be nothing more than myths or exaggerations in the minds of certain viewers, as they warn them of a real product, people are inclined to believe their fellow friends and culture.

That's when influencers shape partnerships to advance the market.

The influencer campaigns aid a lot in the process.

The trust gained makes the industry grow, after all, marketing is based on winning consumer confidence so let's get the consumers to interact with the advertisement.

- **A Far smoother**

  Marketing influencer is a much easier and simpler way to market than digital ad marketing.

  Not only is the way people are drawn easier, but the way it is ultimately placed up doesn't take much work other than the artistic aspect.

  Throughout this age, where all is rendered easier by the media, networking networks and online services have enabled efficient marketing a realizable mission.

  You write about it and share it online and thousands of people will be peeking at your forums and newspapers within minutes.

The online facility helps connect people from around the world.

- **Demand Is rising quicker**

In addition to being a simpler form of marketing, marketing influencer helps boost markets at a high rate.

They will find it as easy as possible, but not easier. — Albert Einstein.

Marketing's influencer approach has the benefit of doing magic online and helps link influencers with people from all over the world.

All questions regarding a product are answered automatically and are usually far more welcomed than an email, ticket comment service, or some other Q&A distribution form.

If it's a social network or a content-driven business, users get responses to all of their queries regarding a company through influencer marketing instantly and even more consider the reviews that render the audience very remarkable.

Throughout the case of social network ads where the commercial is put on all the often-used web networks, consumers get to hear about certain public views, which significantly allows them to weigh up their buying decisions.

Besides that, they are often linked to many people on social media (which in this case serves as influencers) who inform them about a lot of things and thus answers other queries.

Throughout the case of the demand guided by the advertising, influencers are already available to address any user queries. This way it removes any doubts about a product.

- **It's strong. Easy Still**

Influencer markets are, in their own way, powerful. It's strong and credible material posted by influencers. They have the ability to gain trust and reliance from citizens, everything that is required.

Thoughts and thoughts are exchanged across influencer channels and also with customers residing miles away stronger connections are established.

"The advertisement foundations are very deep for every social network, and are not easy to sever."

- **The Scriptures Will Do Miracles**

All those bloggers, journalists, content writers, out there CEOs portray the market accurately through their writings that depend on many consumers' proofs, opinions, and ideas.

These pieces of writing are much more convincing than a few pictures and slogans composed of digital ads. The writings talk of certain people and influencers' feedbacks and views and is a consistency that definitely lags behind on the demand for multimedia advertising. We just could have seen the digital advertising and ads market peak.

- **The Visual Benefit**

  As the social network is loaded with videos of the goods, multimedia advertising that typically consists of banners and posters have become even less influential.

  Live objects are more desirable than still alive, naturally. Influencers have been utilizing videos in their ads to influence the people that turned out to be another plus point in influencer marketing.

- **Influencer Personalities**

  Consumers are highly affected when their favorite celebrities tweet regarding a certain commodity.

  It has become an increasing field of influencer marketing that uses celebrities as influencers to draw people to a particular product. Unlike TV advertisements, where actors are used as influencers, they are today made influencers on social media where they talk about how they have been the consumers of a single company.

This practice doesn't even require any convincing because when their favorite celebrity buys it, many people blindly believe in the quality of the thing.

No wonder, influencer marketing is taking over.

- **Feedback online**

  The consumer's feedbacks are really relevant for marketing purposes as the influencer audience is on social media. The demand is rising for constructive reviews and likewise, it is declining while the input is not in the products and services' favor.

  Citizens today are strongly investing in user reviews and public views.

  The idea of online reviews and engagement fuels influencer marketing and is, therefore, increasing rapidly.

- **Honest Views**

  Consumers trust their views and thoughts more than advertising.

  In the field of influencer marketing, people's opinions are just as relevant and serve as influencers on social sites.

  If not all then most people's feedbacks and views on a particular service or product are real.

  You may purchase the product by getting honest opinions about a subject, an individual, or a business.

  In the case of digital advertising promotion, there are hardly any views exchanged since such contact is not permitted by the ad platform.

- **Efficient Period**

Influencer marketing is immediate and is focused solely on the partnership formed between the influencer and their network.

The idea that marketing influencer takes over digital advertising may only happen now.

It was predicted that marketing will sweep over all the other business methods in a couple more years and become the main marketing activity by 2020.

Chapter 5

Finding the Right Home Business Model for You

Your efforts to find a successful business model for making money on the internet when working from home are likely to always be ongoing work. The bad news: there's no surefire way to make money on the web; the good news: you should try a lot of models.

People are constantly finding new ways to play with tactics and discovering business models that do well for them. Really the solution is a no-brainer. If that doesn't work, then fix it. If you don't have that business model going for you then change it. If you don't see the gains the current model will offer, then it's time to try something different. Some people may not agree but it's just a matter of staying alive; for me-failure is not a choice. Every day new ways of succeeding on the web are being tried and new tools are being offered as you discover. The focus changes, e.g., just going after desktop clients, you've got to get to mobile clients now too. Companies turn from "strong ads" and rely more on advertising on social media.

I term them the ALM of the company model: Here are a few things you need to know about:

- A = Attract Clients.

    If you've spent any time in the Internet Marketing space, you'll have noticed that these days "anything goes" to attract customers. There are hyped up deals all over the web, making amazing claims. That's not the way you want to go, do you? Then you ought to care about the value that the buyers would be getting. There are infinite ways of utilizing goods and/or services to provide interest.

You have to choose the goods either by producing them on your own or by selling the products of others as an affiliate marketer. In reality, making your own product isn't as overwhelming as it may seem since you can outsource almost everything about product development. A creative idea and some time and money are all you need. It's not as straightforward to choose an affiliate company there's a large range of those on the market-as some make it: it's necessary to carefully research and select any company. You'll need to think about the competition of the numerous industry niches you may be moving towards. Yet testing here is certainly more valuable than interminable research.

- L = Leads: Future customers/buyers need to get there.

There are two methods to get leads: by creating free traffic or paying traffic to your company (that you sell presumably on a website). You may be sick with both the free (organic, SEO = search engine optimization) method to traffic marketing and the paying (advertising) method. Then you'll need to set up a mechanism to protect the leads, such as an auto-responder program where the visitors' email addresses to your web or blog are stored.

The autoresponder lets you arrange your leads or "subscribers" daily or occasional follow-up mails; this will allow you to develop a relationship with your prospects.

- M = Monetarising the program

  When traffic arrives at the product lines, you'll start having revenue and earnings. There are tons of opportunities to maximize how you're getting your company plan cost. One of the most relevant rules that you can adopt is "monitor, monitor, measure," i.e. chart the effects of each update, each ad, each market you're involved with, and then make the improvements and modifications.

  Yeah, go ahead and submit the business idea! The downside will be just learning and researching, then never taking any measure.

Developing Social Media Content When You're a Small Business

We also recently discussed some of the most common social networking sites for a small company. A company blog, Facebook, and Twitter were the focal points. We'll dig into content marketing approaches for certain channels next week.

Many of those working with small businesses tend to bear several hats and don't have a full-time copy writer's privilege. Hopefully, you've got someone on your staff that can do some writing. If not, we'll explore some of the options for you in a moment.

Phase One: Be an Expert

Offer the consumers and prospective customers any consideration about what sort of content will be useful. What kind of information do you hold they don't? Obviously, you don't want all of your trade secrets to be given away. Yet at the same time, if the consumers don't have an interest in the material, it won't be successful in catching their attention.

Let's say that we're a flower nursery and that our main business strategy is to offer bulbs, trees, and shrubs. Don't just talk about their particular goods. If you can also write around the periphery of your business, your content will be even stronger — a great technique for not giving away all of your knowledge for free. The material has to appeal to your company, but that will open up the doors to far more possibilities than if you restrict yourself to just your core industry. Any plot suggestions may be "Knowing when to fertilize your lawn" or "Grasses growing good in Kansas"

Build a collection of potential ideas on the plot. It is a perfect opportunity to share thoughts. Think about seasonal problems. Large topics in the industry. And of course, stories related to specific products of yours. Whenever fresh plot suggestions come to mind, submit them to the register. Many of them you will never get around to turning into usable material, but the process of brainstorming and creating lists may help create new subjects to write about.

Phase Two: Web Creation Across the Network

And now you have chosen how to represent yourself as an authority in your profession, and you have created a collection of new ideas for storytelling. Now give some attention to how the content can be spread through various channels. Should you have a business newsletter, either an e-mail or a paper version? When not, it's a perfect chance to start making so. You will be producing content already, and the newsletters will remain an important way to promote your brand. It's not social networking so we continue to find opportunities to function together as small business individuals. And posting content through various channels in marketing and social networking is a major use of our limited capital.

And we've agreed to compose an article for our nursery on what kinds of plants grow under intense sunshine that flower during the summer months. (Can you tell me I was gardening this past weekend?) We'll compose a longer version of this content for our newsletter — anywhere from ten to twenty paragraphs of detail. That fits in well with the printed newsletter from our business. Keep the content updated and not sales. When you may, it is OK to offer it a little flavor, but the idea is to create material that would be beneficial to your customers.

Once that is finished, the content will now be cannibalized for the remainder of the advertising needs. Whether the material is not too long you can include it on your site, or condense it to a duration that is more user-friendly. Using the first few paragraphs of your e-newsletter, with a link to your website's full post. Post any short quips on your Facebook account — you might also be able to grab a couple of short quips so you can share material from the same tale on many separate times on Facebook. And eventually, tweets need a few really brief quips.

That's a great tactic I'd name your key content for. Spend a couple of hours writing an essay, and using it all over your advertising channels. But also you may need to create some shorter material for your social channels.

Phase 3: Quick Hits

You'll need to mix it into your social media in a few clicks. This is the perfect location to show your personality. In your Facebook posts and messages, if your newsletter needs to be a little more intense, let your hair hang out a little. Comment on special stuff happening at your service. You might be excited about a new product and would like to share a photo and a short explanation. Maybe you want to let people know about a special award you've got, or you're interested in a civic effort. And maybe you like to just hear TGIF!

Let me send you a brief bit of advice: customers choose the ones they want to do business with. Let them know you better through your posts and tweets. Let them see a certain character and a certain attitude.

Help! Help! I'm not able to write!

And you mean you're not allowed to write? And no one on your staff would want to do that either? There are possibilities. If there is a college in your city, in the journalism department, make friends with somebody. Students in college require training and always come in free. Look around the neighborhood, a lot of freelance writers usually operate from home. Are you a leader of some trade organizations? They can have channels from which to purchase content. And there are other online writing forums where you can post your needs to become a professional researcher.

Chapter 6

Common Mistakes in Social Media Marketing

Social media marketing is perhaps the most talked-about marketing strategy in today's economic implementation. However, most people make the mistake of believing that social networking is simple and easy but the truth is-it's not that easy as it seems. Social media is a platform that can make your image or authenticity among customers. If it's adequately used it can improve company ROI along with brand awareness. Below will evaluate the 10 major mistakes that one makes when doing social media marketing.

1. No proper strategy or schedule — Before you begin with your company promotion or advertising; it's essential to have a clear objective or goal i.e. what are the result from this marketing and how to achieve these strategic goals. Make a clear statement of all these points and adopt them.

2. Not understanding the platform/medium that you are using — It's critical to know your business and selecting the right platform to get the targeted audience. Do a detailed investigation of these mediums and list down the benefits to target the right audience.

3. Giving less importance to your blog — Your company blog can be a good platform to have user interest content all of the time. Here you got an opportunity to connect with the

specific groups. Place all your business social media sites on the blog.

4. Inconsistent Marketing — Regular updates are important. From time to time updates and proper engagement will assist in building buzz and the information will be viral. In this, just be authentic in every interaction and promote your product as honestly as possible.

5. No Proper Engagement — There are further sub-points to be discussed in this. These are as follows:

    a. No replies on time: You don't feel good about waiting for any answer to your question or comment. If you don't even get a comment it hurts even worse. Therefore, make sure the questions on your sites are addressed.

    b. No recording of your stats: In marketing campaigns statistics are important. But make sure you keep records of every operation you carry out over these mediums.

    c. Too much involvement: Too much of it can even destroy your company. Having posts with needless posts in each second will offend the follower. Be original, without imposing the follower on anything.

6. Effective 24/7: Not required! Make a time — slot of it when you can target the highest number of target customers to meet them on schedule.

7. Using social media platforms only for engagement and not for sales or lead generation — Engagement is the primary job but nobody has stopped you for not making any sales pitch or lead generation opportunity. If there's a (real) possibility then go for it.

8. Simple is Boring — Creativity is always praised and inventions are always valued. Make your page creatively interactive and in an honest manner.

9. Not keeping an eye on the competitors — keep a check on them at all times, will help you make the right strategy and keep you ahead of your competitors.

10. Fearful of getting derogatory feedback —Nobody to want blunt or offensive remarks. But these comments are faced in social media; this negative feedback will help you learn about your weak links, and you can improve later on.

Social media allows you to connect with your customers directly and effectively spread the word of mouth. So, social networking is the perfect way to encourage business and a cost-efficient approach is to optimize returns.

What to Do while Selling on Your Social Media

Social media such as Facebook, Twitter, Myspace, and LinkedIn are just some of the other social media networks that can be identified and used to sell real estate on the internet. Having an account and making usage of it will give you an advantage over your competitors. But, agents sometimes committed mistakes in using these social media that lead to losing their potential clients without even knowing it.

To avoid losing your potential customers and maximize the returns from these social networking sites. You have to avoid the mistakes most real estate agents commonly make. Below you can see the compilation of some of the errors commonly made by the police.

Note that the Facebook profile page is not for a company with your mates. As I have observed that more and more real estate agents have their profile pages, they likely contain their personal information along with business information. If you are an official, it is not correct to publicly post your personal information, especially if you post images of your wife, children, grandchildren, or relatives. The solution to this problem is to create a group of password codes for your personal information, making your profile page in Google unsearchable. Facebook has a fan page and marketplace area where you can post your home listings, open house, or any information about real estate marketing. It will surface publicly after publishing there and can be checked through Google in this manner you will have an opportunity to improve your search engine ranking.

Users don't want to read materials about real estate every day. Social media members are interested in meeting people of the same interest and having a conversation. Print and web advertising are special but this kind of error is made by most real estate agents. They use social media as much as they do in print media feeding people with a bunch of real estate's marketing materials that they are not interested in and would like to have. Every advertisement has its purpose, social media is based on engagement, while print media is intended to create people's awareness.

A huge mistake to invite others to be a fan of yours. I think this is the biggest mistake the agent has to avoid, to create his/her own fan page, and to invite others to be their fan. Do not promote yourself, when you send someone to tell them you've become a fan of yourself, it's just like relaying a message that tells them "hey watch out and read my own testimonials." The smart thing to do is to use the Facebook fan page to share facts regarding the regional audience you are targeting, why they will see that region, and how pleasant life in that region is. You can get more real estate customers in that way.

There are plenty of ways to get it right and wrong when it comes to social media marketing. Hopefully, these little tips from my will help you think through your tactics on social media. Generally, these social media mistakes will serve as your guide in your recent and future social media marketing.

Avoid These 3 Mistakes in Social Media Marketing

The Cluetrain Manifesto claims that "Markets are Conversations." The Manifesto is a document that was published in 1999 and 10 years later is still considered to be an outstanding Internet phenomenon treatise-in terms of the impact and opportunities of Internet and web technology on the modern businessman. This assertion has nowhere been borne out more than in the complex, fascinating social media marketing (SMM) world. Any definition of SMM requires an understanding of social media networks. These are any community-driven networks focused on content created by users. Of starters, the primary goal of YouTube is to display user-generated content, not to advertise the goods from the parent corporation. Networks on social media include Twitter, Facebook, Reddit, and many others.

Therefore SMM is the use of these channels to promote and market to the intended audience of the promoter products, services, or information. This could be a traditional product looking for a market, for example, an author promoting a new novel. Or it might be something much bigger; the US presidential election of 2008 brought Twitter into the spotlight as a way for the aspirants to quickly transmit a message to the target audience, helping keep them updated on happenings on the trail. In the latter case, no tangible product was being promoted per se, but it was a means of promoting the candidates and their messages. Twitter exploded in popularity following the election and remains a current subject of debate.

The smart Business Strategy should seek to understand these possibilities and reach out to the available social media platforms to reach their customers directly. However, SMM does have as many drawbacks as rewards. Many politicians have made official their tweets, so they regret it. Here are a few simple errors to make, and how to prevent them.

Mistake #1 — *Not Having a Blog*

Anybody's got a forum. Although that may not necessarily be valid, interpretation is certainly true. Free services such as WordPress and BlogSpot provide an organized and attractive form of voice for anyone with a connection. Twitter, Facebook, and other networks are helpful but are not under the direct control of a customer. But a blog is, and the savvy marketer will benefit from that. A user can post his views, observations, and opinions in a blog with very little constraint and go into more depth than most social networks require. For example, Twitter only allows posts of 140 characters, which is surely too small to describe a product or dissected a major political speech. However, a brief 'tweet' reminding book fans that a blog interviewed their favorite author would bring people flocking to the web where they will not only read the interview but also potentially the many other posts on the site.

This of course means reliable blogging is successful blogging. A blog can't be overlooked and posted even when major events happen — Internet users' current attention period is relatively short. To order to keep bringing to their target audience, bloggers need to regularly publish strong content; not month by month but also day by day.

Mistake #2 — *Don't Mark Yourself*

The internet is an ocean of knowledge and for people to regularly consider a commodity or a business is a struggle. The smart online marketer will take advantage of the opportunity to sell their name with every opportunity to network. When a corporation has a forum and a website for the commodity, they need to communicate. The blog has to support the key objective of the web, and the web has to direct visitors to its excellent blog material. Social networking posts will link to this 'name' image, and keep the message clear across all of them. The successful SMM strategy views each product as a single entity and consistently manages them. Each tweet on Twitter, each post on Facebook will alert people who are sharing the material and where they can find more.

Mistake #3 — Not Being good

As already stated, "Markets Are Conversations." Web consumers are not machines. When a certain combination of parameters is added, they will respond with a pre-programmed action. We are people with thoughts who thought independently, so we got used to getting their say. Although a marketer needs to take every chance to spread his message, that doesn't mean dragging him into any discussion. Participants on social networking platforms will easily recognize other marketers' more ham-fisted attempts and let their friends know of their disappointment. A negative name will travel easily on the Web-a certain St. Louis police officer lost his career after Facebook uploaded a photo showing the cop violating his power.

The best strategy, then, is not to treat such areas as locations to sell, nor locations to converse. Only showing up on Facebook and uploading a new product to every possible community is a fast way to get recognized and dismissed as incompetent. On the other side, a member might enter many groups with talks about their personal interests, developing friendships, and credibility as a professional commentator. Instead, they're more apt to be taken literally as they direct people to their blog. Clear courtesy and community appreciation will go a long way to achieving any further hits per message.

Like in every other communication strategy, SMM essentially needs preparation, patience, and logical thinking. It is not a short series of clever commercials that can be aired for several months at a time, but a means of consistently communicating, day in and day out, with a target audience. Strong SMM will have regular, relevant material for its target audiences and be prepared to engage in a ton of give-and-take for an audience ideally suited to having their opinions known.

Chapter 7

Local Marketing — Branch Out with this Advice

Local marketing is the backbone or pillar of any successful small business company, those businessmen who have chosen to ignore it, pay the highest price by struggling to get their business off the ground or stagnating in a state with marginal companies that are also listed.

What Is Local Marketing?

Local or Locality Marketing is defined as pinpoint or location awareness, generated within a given and restricted geographic area, thereby emphasizing a particular spot, point, or destination for consumers who eventually become customers to locate your company. Or else listed as, bringing you and your company on the globe.

Why We Need to Target Locality

Locality Marketing is known as a 'Below the Line' marketing effort, Below the Line sale promotion is an immediate or delayed opportunity to purchase, conveyed in cash or rewards or kind, and typically short-lived. It is an incredibly efficient and cost-effective approach for reaching a small and unique group near your business premises.

What sustain you, in the long run, is the Primary Market, why is that?

1. Consumers are close to you, they work in the area and they live there.

2. With greater ease you can measure your marketing efforts and your success.

3. As an entrepreneur, you normally belong to the same consumer community.

4. Users are clients; in the end, customers are mates.

5. When the company gains momentum, this naturally negates the usual risks associated with a start-up business.

There are various media and local marketing firms that offer you the job choice to help your awareness efforts, and in future books, we will focus on those.

A unique Marketing Effort — Neighborhood

The environment and global warming implications are topical and important, but limited or negligible, future and existing customers are all informed of this topical issue as a business owner, you may have an opportunity to make an impact.

A recommendation is to get involved in your botanical neighborhood to gain credibility from naturalists and all climate mavens. Trees are the most vital part of our biosphere due to their ability to convert carbon dioxide into oxygen.

Adopt all of the community's vital or noticeable and larger trees, turning such actions into what can then be known as the community or, more aptly, "neighborhood" how is this achieved?

Compass points in a circle area (about two or three miles from your company) take the trees, a prime example: (the huge old oak at the intersection of Jack Avenue and Jones Street), take trees at all the compass points surrounding your business, and you get a broad range of acceptance.

Approach your local council or municipality and offer the trees you have identified and selected on their behalf to be supported and nurtured, so you become the official keeper of the selected trees.

Place small billboards or plaques next to the trees, promote your company, and own portion of the branch.

Use the trees in all potential promotional content and mediums as history charts.

Plant trees in your primary market on Arbor Day, and send them to the society, get free press for such activities. The press is freely enjoying nature and goodwill tales.

Enter networks, associations, and restoration projects to become a protector of all botanical issues in your primary area.

Sponsor old-style swinging cradles in your primary sector, this encourages a sense of reverence and affection for trees in children from an early age, and the neighborhood would be thankful for your participation in outdoor events with their babies.

Arrange talks on trees and their benefits to the planet at elementary schools, this is a subtle form of advertising for your business on a platform not often used, and less commercial or garish in its appearance.

Global vs. Local Marketing — Which Approach Is Right for Your Small Business?

Because of the new introduction of local search algorithms by Google, there has been a lot of talk around local marketing lately. If you have a small business website, you might be uncertain about what it all entails and what path you can take. Here are some details that can help to clear things up for you.

Before adding local search, what you had to do was bring the website online, perform any SEOs to be listed in the search engines, and then basically advertise the website. Wins the platform with the best SEO tactics. Now it's a little more complicated but at the same time better if you know what's required to achieve performance.

What Is Local Search, and What Is It Like?

It basically means that if I am from the United Kingdom and I search for a digital camera, Google will place all websites that are optimized for digital cameras and are located in the United Kingdom ahead of any other websites in the search results it gives me. The reason that I would probably prefer to buy locally and that websites from my own country are more relevant to my needs.

This indicates that if you include local marketing or geo-targeting as part of your SEO strategy, you are much more likely to get a good placement in the search engines. If you do business strictly within your own country, then local marketing will be very important to you. Otherwise, your website may never be viewed by your target audience.

If you're doing business internationally, you're going to want to include a combination of global and local marketing strategies to optimize your online exposure and attract as much new business as possible. By using local SEO techniques, you'll be able to use keywords that target specific regions and countries that you know are most open to your products and services.

Let's say I knew Canadians were big buyers of digital cameras, then I might want to register a.ca domain name, host my website on a Canadian web hosting service, and include some SEO strategies that would target the Canadian market. Although I'm located in the UK, I still can use local marketing techniques to appear in the local search when someone from Canada searches for me.

So what's the answer to the local vs global question and what's right for your business? The answer is local but for some, it means global-local marketing.

Capture the Local Market with low-Cost Marketing

For companies seeking to increase their market share, there are a few simple and straightforward strategies to improve local marketing without breaking the bank. Also, most small to medium-sized organizations need to be able to maximize limited budgets. This means increasing the company's identity through marketing approaches that lower the cost of finding customers.

Flyers and Flipcharts

One of the more common marketing strategies is to use flyers and leaflet drops, where consumers are given a flyer in person, or a collection of client flyers and leaflets are distributed via mail or courier. Leaflet drops have been a staple in local marketing approaches for decades, offering businesses a simple solution to get a message across to buyers.

To Become a Member of the City Chamber of Commerce

Any prospective customers will probably look for products and services from a local chamber of commerce website or blog. Securing a connection to a chamber of commerce website or blog is an economical way to promote a local business. Other strategies involve securing links to similar or comparable companies in the same region. Nevertheless, do not avoid securing a link.

TV Advertisements and Fundraisers

An extremely effective way of promoting a local business is to advertise on a local radio station and or hold a fundraiser and event promotion to benefit a local charity or community need. It's a proactive approach to local marketing that allows businesses to get upfront with their community, their people, and potential customers.

It's always best to keep things simple and straightforward when it comes to local marketing. Companies seeking to increase their exposure in a local market need not invest lavishly delivering outcomes. Find these three as inexpensive marketing strategies for promoting a local business.

Use AdWords Geo-Targeting to Improve local Marketing Results

If you've been in the SEO game for a while now, you know there are a lot of different ways to achieve the outcomes you're looking for. SEO is interpreted in many different ways and everyone seems to decide "what's right." But, for your advertising money, there are tangible paths that you can take to ensure you get a good ROI. One such avenue is via AdWords.

Local marketing experts know that geo-targeting their PPC campaign ads is the key to achieving success in a local paid marketing quest. Few companies have physical locations locally run that use geo-targeted AdWords campaigns to bring more consumers through the front door. Many businesses are bigger enterprises of local retail stores looking to drive sales by promoting their specific locations' performance. The idea behind geo-targeting was, in nature, always social. The aim is to create more companies through geo-targeting paying ad campaigns to specific locations.

One of the main issues local marketing search experts notice is that the Google AdWords campaigns are not set to a specific area by default. Many business owners do not understand this part of paid search marketing, so they end up spending extra money excessively on clicks from users outside the serviceable client area of their business.

Recommended Settings Are Analyzed

Google AdWords recommends by default the settings which will send as many clicks as possible to a website. Recommended settings for Google are not geo-targeting and a concentrated effort. They are for click generation. For the most part, local marketing experts and local businesses have little or no use for visitors outside of their intended area. They are unlikely to reach clients outside of a particular area for most small companies, and so the clicks coming from beyond their serviceable zone result in needless expenditure on AdWords.

Using the current Google AdWords configuration makes sense in certain cases. Only sites without a physical location wish to serve a national or global customer base. Local companies with an easily shippable product could also direct their paid ad campaigns on targeted as well as non-targeted terms.

Using Geo-Configurations

It's not the wrong decision to use the accessible Google AdWords geo-targeting settings, which in certain instances can generate convenience which functional clicks and traffic. Most company owners should be relatively happy with the outcomes by utilizing only the geo-targeting settings open. It'll take local marketing experts a step further. The safest method is to use, implement, and check geo-targeted variables. Be sure to produce a regional report to explain the effect of utilizing the Google AdWords settings open, or not.

When the geo settings available include an appropriate amount of non-local traffic otherwise the choice will be taken to actually use the settings available. Nonetheless, if the settings are available for too many non-local clicks, then a more sophisticated solution is needed. At this stage, local marketing search experts will get extra granular on keyword research levels to determine and optimize the best approach for leveraging the Google AdWords campaign for business locally.

The Partnership Between Website Ownership and Local Marketing Performance

In fact, owning a website is a good thing for business but what matters, in the end, is how successful the website is. How is a Website's success measured? A website's effectiveness is calculated in many respects but the most significant aspect is the degree of interaction that it establishes between prospective clients and the company owner.

Taking up some sort of strategy for mobile marketing or local marketing strategies is something that requires careful consideration. One such factor is to have a successful website. The first step towards a successful local marketing campaign is to run a website that can promote the products and services of the business owner and also give him or her full hold on the marketing messages that are being sent.

When a business owner is able to reach his or her local market, the person has the opportunity to educate the targeted prospective customers of who he or she is, and what kind of products or services they should expect and would have. If you can do this through your website, gain control over your marketing messages, then it is said that successful marketing has occurred.

A company owner will also realize that the two most crucial items to hold in mind when carrying out some sort of marketing are to attract new customers and, second, to do anything possible to keep these consumers going back to the website to make their potential purchases.

Another way a website will help with successful local marketing is by personalizing the site, either using mobile marketing strategies or local marketing strategies. Only by opting for a custom-made platform will one do that, which can help one educate his or her clients of the details they need about the company owner and the goods and services being provided.

Local Marketing Tips for Online Entrepreneurs

It's nice to draw people to your Website. Marketing is an integral aspect of making progress online. But if you don't market to the right people, your efforts are going to be for naught. Here are some tips to help you use your marketing efforts to reach your local market:

Through the search engine optimization projects, using long-tail keywords. In many cases, these phrases refer to local locations and niche specialties and can help you target your local demographic, rather than fighting against the much larger competition base trying to rank for short-tail keywords. A good example of this is the attempt to rank Cheshire's pizza parlor instead of pizza or UK marketing consultancy rather than marketing. Your target as your competition narrows

Customer/prospect has more chance to find what they are looking for.

Mind the Market

Understanding who you're up to in the online marketing environment will help make your target audience more attractive. If you are a hotel, then you can try to appeal to the local area and also try to appear to the clients of your biggest competitor. Understanding what would not go well for your rivals might allow you to overtake them.

Directories Central

Getting listed in local directories will do many things for you. It helps local directory browsers find you and helps search engines connect the dots between your geographic area, your business niche, and your target clients. Directory submissions will help you boost targeted traffic rates and organic SEO, particularly when targeted by local geographical region and niche.

Local marketing should be about more than just greeting guests as they arrive at the website. Try to catch such leads via marketing authorization strategies or, for example, by a sales pipeline with autoresponder tools. You can not only work on turning visitors into real customers but if they are local, this might also help you with local referrals. There's a lot you can do to gradually increase your market share in your area!

Global Commercialization

For local businesses, social marketing is great. They can find people to follow based on geographic area, advertise to their customers, use data mining techniques to learn more about their audience, niche, and competition, and use that to build their brand and strengthen their relationships. If you don't use social media resources like Twitter or Facebook, you may be losing out!

Local marketing strategies will dramatically help you develop your company. And there are consultants who can provide you with a customized strategy if you need help.

Chapter 8

Social Media Marketing and Article Copywriting

Social media marketing has rendered online business opportunities more common. It all began as a grassroots movement that has evolved into a successful platform to support companies, goods, and services. Corporate organizations are moving gradually towards using social media and profiting from its positive effects. Net networking as a refresher relies on a more beneficial relationship for company partners, future clients, and current consumers.

Both major and minor players should endeavor to understand the crucial marketing responsibilities of social media. In reality, it plays an important role in marketing that depends on the company and whether it better fits the venture's requirements. This always depends on the commitment an individual chooses to make in the social networking field.

Social Media Strategies to Consider

One of the questions that should be answered is can companies ignore strategies for social media marketing as an effective way of advertising their products and services? This cannot be replied to automatically and it will be best to see the outcomes or changes in the year ahead.

Due to the idea of social media marketing, networking in the industry has never become more expedient than it is today. Ascertain search engine optimization analysts accurately put it, market opportunities are only one button ahead. Social networks keep attracting so many people who could end up becoming your future contacts.

Copywriting As an Offline Opportunity

Digital copywriting is among the electronic market prospects currently growing in terms of volume. It is different from conventional copywriting, although the purpose of properly implemented copywriting marketing is to increase the online presence of business ventures. It aims to foster awareness and motivation among target audiences.

Those are the variables in copywriting that should always be considered:

The content has to be capable of capturing the target audience's interest through the article title.

The headline will inspire readers and fuel their curiosity.

A DAY IN THE LIFE OF A COPYWRITER

Median Wage: $61,820 per year

Produce error free content

AD
Write prose for advertising purposes

Manage multiple projects

Interpret creative direction

the balance

The material has to be meaningful and give the readers practical information.

Copywriting is primarily intended to win over readers to become loyal customers and to patronize your goods or services.

Keep in mind that it is not website design and advanced technologies that matter but the fact that the copy of the website should be sufficiently persuasive. To be successful, the site must be able to generate substantial traffic. SEO copywriting can enhance website ranking by placing keywords on the web pages at the correct locations and in the middle of tabs. The web pages must, of course, be appropriate and capable of connecting to readers as well as persuading readers and search engine spiders alike.

The first pointer about SEO copywriting is that it focuses on generating content that is valuable to online users while at the same time achieving better search engine rankings. The next suggestion is to avoid web page cramming with keywords and keyword phrases that don't work out. Because of irrelevant content, those websites may be blocked. With the aid of search engine optimization, the information can be made relevant.

Today, there are too many business opportunities online that help people who need extra revenue to earn money without needing to leave their homes.

SEO Copywriters — How to Pick a Platform for Social Network Ads

Marketing on social media is here to live. That being said, every SEO copywriter needs to make a part of their regular marketing routine in particular. Why? If you are a copywriter with SEO, many of your customers are online. So, that's where you do need to be clear.

Plus, there are too many social networking advertisement platforms to pick from. How are you picking the best one and make things work for you? Below are two critical guidelines that will help you narrow down the field.

Copywriters SEO: 2 critical Items to Keep in Mind When Selecting a Communications Platform for Social Media

Have you got the time? If you do so correctly, social media marketing is time-consuming. So you need to pick a format that fits with the amount of time you need to devote to it.

After all, there is no sense in using an outlet if you are not going to invest time fully in it.

If you're a busy SEO writer-as many tend to be-you won't have hours for a community to interact with. Therefore a social media marketing tool such as Twitter might be ideal for you. Since you have only 140 characters to tell what you want, your posts/answers are supposed to be quick and simple by nature.

On Twitter, you can post 5, 10, or 20 times a day — in just a few minutes. That makes it a perfect outlet if you are continually pressed for time.

Objective: What is your aim to participate in social media marketing as an SEO copywriter? Of course, the ultimate aim is still attracting more customers; taking in more profits.

Yet, are you doing so publicly, or clandestinely? That is the argument. Some social networking advertisement channels are more suited for direct messaging (such as LinkedIn), whereas some are more of a way to remain tuned in and available (such as Twitter).

When picking a social media marketing platform, make sure that the goal fits with it well. Otherwise, you can do more harm than good to your freelance writing business.

Common Platforms for Social Media Marketing

Then are four extremely popular social media marketing outlets and their demographic overall.

- **LinkedIn:** For professionals to use more.

- **Twitter:** Used by everyone along also a number of internet businessmen, writers, Twitter marketers, and so on.

- **MySpace:** MySpace has around 122 million users, according to social media marketing experts. They vary from rock stars to mass industry. It is used by many for social purposes, as well as for business.

- **Facebook:** The College crowd made it popular. You can notice a combination close to that of MySpace here.

- **The Bottom Line:** Social networking marketing is a perfect opportunity for SEO copywriters-and other web marketers-to stay unobtrusively in front of prospective clients. But, you have to invest time in it and not misuse it to get the business in.

Chapter 9

How to Promote Your Brand with Social Media

There's something remarkable going on here today. Content no longer works the way it used to. The idea of buying some TV time or placing an ad in a newspaper was previously considered smart and effective, but nowadays, most people especially the youth, spend a lot of their idle time socializing on the internet and even getting their news online. This isn't an inherently odd phenomenon as man has been a social being since the beginning of time. What is unprecedented, though, is the rapid rate at which communication has been enhanced by the widespread use of the Internet which today creates our virtual reality.

There were more than 1 billion Facebook users, more than 200 million active users, and also accessible in 35 different languages as of March 2013. More than 346 million people worldwide are reading blogs and 184 million are bloggers themselves. Facebook has more than 200 million registered users who post an average of 3 million messages per day together, and YouTube boasts about 100 million viewers each month. In more than 200 countries and territories, LinkedIn has more than 200 million members.

It is not all doom and gloom, however. You don't have to try to outspend the biggest companies to promote your brand anymore; now you are outsmarting them with viral videos. You don't have to spend thousands on sterile focus groups; with quick Twitter searches, you get the pulse of your market at your fingertips. The social media world is an excellent place to reach existing customers, extend your access to new markets, and maintain good relations with other brands.

Today it's possible for anyone to build and, most critically, share their own material through the advent of new web technologies. A blog post, tweet, Facebook page, or YouTube video can virtually be produced and viewed for free by millions. Advertisers do not need to spend large amounts of money for delivering advertising advertisements to advertisers or publishers; instead, they may produce advertising own compelling material to which audiences flock. Further, people are linked than ever and any second the company doesn't involve them in social networking is a loss of potential. So, get on track.

Until we begin, let's juggle our minds about identifying some main words. The media can be described simply as a forum for exchanging ideas. Traditional outlets, such as TV, newspapers, radio, and magazines, are one-way, stagnant advertising systems that are becoming less successful communication tools today. Unlike its predecessor, social media is a new platform where we can share ideas; say things that we like and don't like; find people who share common interests, etc. Online networking sources cover forums, LinkedIn, Instagram, Pinterest, and Google+.

Considering the following as minor tactics to support the brand via social media:

- **Be Real and authentic**

  Social media should be used to market your physical identity as a virtual medium. Even because your actual identity is real, so must your computer identity be special too. Being genuine offers you continuity with your consumers which will encourage brand loyalty and increasing the happiness of the consumers. This is true because most people buy other than vice-versa from who they like and trust. Social networking offers you the ability to exchange information and by leveraging it correctly, you can help create trust in your company by showing other people the importance of your business.

- **Live Outside**

  Social networking is about transparency and communication. Businesses looking to develop a brand online will first identify consumers and keep engaging them in discussions that educate their customers about their products. These conversations should be two-way between the companies and their customers to ensure both parties have adequate feedback. Companies ought to be alert, as such discussions are already taking place at the front of millions of individuals, and they will be recorded for years to come.

- **Be alive, and Take Action**

Social networking facilitates real-time contact between the various parties concerned. For news to appear is not an uncommon experience and has already been propagated on social networking sites before they appear on the traditional news media like newspapers and TV. Customers likewise enjoy these days if you can respond to their concerns and problems as rapidly as possible Failure to react on time could leave your competitors scrambling for alternative solutions.

- **Track your Brand**

Whether you are a local business or an international brand, people on the Internet may already be thinking about you. Yet you've got to continue learning before you can get interested in those discussions. You will start referring to what is being said, where it is being said, and who is doing it when you start listening. However, monitoring social media should be an ongoing process, and you should take advantage of different social media platforms to ensure that nothing slips through the cracks

– the right (or wrong) story can come from anywhere and burst into your face. You're not trying to get caught off guard.

- **Spread Your Word**

Your own "mouth word" is the greatest weapon for marketing. Tell everyone. Thanks! Tell all your families, family, and employers that you are launching a social networking push and publicly widening your consumer quest. The more people hear of this groundbreaking venture, the more probable your prospective consumers' ears would be passed on to the press. The best advertising you can get is free so make sure you maximize all of the free advertising you can get.

How to Enhance Your Social Networking Site/Blog

We all know that blogs are incredibly effective resources, particularly for businesses in this era of social media marketing. Blogs are loved by search engines and customers. They're insightful, their material is often new, and they encourage companies to have their customers customized. Nevertheless, none of this necessarily works if people cannot locate your blog. That also seems to be humanity's downfall. We enjoy the concept of the surface level just don't dive far enough to find out the details of how all this operates.

With your blog configuration, you have now found a big problem: no traffic. Your words are worthless without the flow. Today, you should start utilizing pure, search engine optimization principles to attract enthusiastic followers. You can always just sit back and hope that you gain a lot of subscribers simply by writing amazing content, but there's another way to gain readers in a more rapid fashion, and that is social media.

Now, remember, we're not just talking about setting up a quick profile page and hoping that the traffic will come to you. That's exactly the same with your blog you're already doing, with absolutely no success! Here are only a few successful moves you may take to attract support for your blog through your social networking activities.

- Create a Relevant Profile — Do not create a personal profile that is completely unrelated to your business blog. You need to determine why you are qualified to discuss your chosen topic with your future "connections" and make it easy for them to find you too. Build your personal profile which will clarify your company a little bit. Creating a separate page for places like Facebook is more business-related and less personal. Branding is walking a fine line while being social so don't overdo it.

- Seek strangers — People don't come to you all the time. You ought to go out to check them out. Many social networks allow this very quickly. Typically you will see people with common preferences when they bring up certain keywords or tags beneath. It can be a little more complicated for Twitter. You'll want to search for Pages that are somehow directly related to the type of business you're in, such as the Page, and start contributing to the content. By that, I don't mean spamming them with your connections, but actively engaging and contributing value to conversations. Soon enough, you can notice people like you and your website and finally click on your blog.

- Stay positive — No one wants a mud ball. When you don't talk and connect, people won't realize that you're in there. If you don't contribute, it will be even more of an insult, and then randomly spam people and pages with the link to your blog. It is considered disrespectful. You wouldn't go to a dance, you wouldn't present yourself to someone and then immediately start giving out your business cards to anyone there.

- Get Site-Specific — Various social networks to have different types of features added. LinkedIn, for example, helps you to link RSS of your blog to your profile. Facebook lets Pages be built. Find out what all of your options are, and take advantage of each.

- Automate — There's plenty of software out there that can help you manage your social media, or at least make life a little easier. These kinds of software can automatically accept requests from friends, respond to requests from friends, send messages to people of similar interest, post status updates, and more. The strategies will also be a bit black-hat, but lookout. Try using software that is intended to automate in a legitimate way.

In reality, the social network and SEO are closer to one another than most businesses know. As customers study your name, goods, and services online, they're not only seeking knowledge across your messages, blogs, and other media chatter-they 're discovering your material that's scattered around the internet and shared through organic search results on other websites.

Google and other engines track and catalog what is happening now on social networks. Search engine crawlers are already browsing and reviewing public Facebook accounts, trending trends on Twitter, blog articles, as well as images, videos, and all kinds of material that get posted and generated on social networking sites. Because of this, managing the social media of your company would significantly profit from utilizing certain SEO know-how for your virtual chats and sharing. Here are four items in the search engine results pages (SERPs) which will make your social network more streamlined and, therefore, more effective.

Choose the Keywords Just As SEO Does

It is important to define your high-value primary focus terms or keywords and phrases in order to maximize any material that is connected with your brand or on your website or social media. Focus on your brand's top 50 to 100 most common and important phrases-too many obscure keywords would ultimately bog down your SEO strategy. Be precise and create a detailed list of the words you plan to achieve.

In Your Blogs, Posts, Use the Keywords, Hashtags, and Ties Liberally

As described above, search engines are certainly indexing tweets-particularly supported ones or those by high profile accounts. Make the most of the chance by using the main words where applicable. Remember, no one wants to hear the same words being repeated over and over you are not a spambot and no follower wants you to sound like one. Only use keywords where it is appropriate and important to do so at the proper time.

Using Your Keywords and Ties and Add Them to Your Blog Titles

As social networking is one of the most common platforms that you can post every form of content your company produces, it makes sense to include your important main words in that edition. Blogs are a perfect way to build and view licensed content and should be the primary place to have a complete influence on what versions, names, and photographs to use. Blog articles that are eventually exchanged via social networking need to be streamlined and keywords in the title, connections, and tags are a strong starting point.

Many social networking platforms let users post details of the material they upload. This not only makes the site more comprehensible and user-friendly for the other users who see your message but also allows search engine crawlers more accessible. Including in-depth explanations using the most relevant keywords in:

- The segment 'about' at your Facebook account

- You segment 'About' on your Twitter profile

- YouTube channel headings and explanations

- Pinterest basics

Social media plays a significant part in any SEO campaign and you can improve the odds of showing up in the SERPs by integrating tried and tested SEO concepts into the social media of the company.

Chapter 10

Dropshipping

Besides being a professional blogger, I also operate my own wholesale and dropshipping company in the UK. But what do you mean by dropshipping, and why do you care?

Dropshipping is a company concept of minimal costs and incredibly small start-ups. It's where a lot of traders get off before they go on to brick-and-mortar shops. Dropshipping implies that you are selling those goods to your own consumer base from a retailer, typically in China. When a consumer orders a drug, you give the order back to the customer to the manufacturer in China, and they "dropship" it. You don't treat the products so you don't need to keep any product.

Wholesale and dropshipping are sometimes lumped together, but in reality dropshipping is significantly lower risk due to not needing to buy any product first. I began dropshipping myself, then went into the wholesale after I had a stronger understanding of the marketing cycle.

What Is It that You Need to Start?

The only thing you need to get going really is a way to advertise the goods. The internet is the obvious alternative but you might also find door-to-door ads or catalog delivery. Obviously, selling door to door or in the local newspaper would take a budget, but it is relatively inexpensive to create a website and advertise online.

In this specific book, I'm not going to discuss the subject of choosing a WebHost but subscribe to my channel and I'm going to seek and compose one early. Suffice it to suggest that you ought to run your own WordPress site or related program at least. I'm sure the free blogger.com or WordPress.com won't cut it — but there are lots of actual website hosting that you can get for as little as $5 a month which is more than appropriate.

There are still a number of various methods for publishing a shop so check about and test out others before you settle on one. Again, in a future post, I will discuss some of those in-depth. If you're struggling to wake up and continue right now, try out shopify.com, which manages the side of the hosting and shopping cart, and they offer a trial of 30 days.

You'll also need to locate a suitable manufacturer for dropshipping (more on this later) and line your new shop with products.

It is pretty much that. You send the same request to the dropship manufacturer anytime a client orders a request, and they ship it for you, directly to the consumer. Checking the manufacturer first to get a feel for the answer times and efficiency is typically a safe feel.

Stuff to Worry About

When exporting merchandise to the UK, there would be customs and import fees on products above a certain amount, please make sure that the client is aware of this. My recommendation is to stick to low-cost products before you have more insight into the company. Some dropshippers can purposely (and illegally) send products classified as a "gift," so customs don't charge buyers, so you need to be alert.

You may still need to file at some stage as a self-employed or a private limited business, so this is a whole different subject. But do not let this scare you off.

Where to Locate a Decent Dealer

Finding a decent supplier is the secret to beginning your dropshipping business on the best foot. I suggest you start with this dropshipping and wholesale site in China, as they list all the best wholesale and dropshipper sites according to a number of factors. Essentially, you are searching for durability, protection, and the number of goods.

That is it! Come back in the future to learn all about the various e-commerce platforms and website hosting out there which will give you the versatility and power you need to develop your new wholesale or dropshipping sector.

How to Use Social Media Marketing for Your Dropshipping Business?

The reality, however, is that many dropship company owners are doing exactly this – building a Facebook profile, or setting up Instagram and Twitter accounts just after they've launched their venture, instead of plunging into a desperate scramble to create a follow-up and make social media function.

Needless to mention, it never does. At least not as it takes that path. This is a matter of too little, too late for most company owners.

If you're going to truly make money dropshipping and really be good at it, you need to incorporate social networking into whatever you're doing right from the get-go.

Platforms such as Twitter, Pinterest, and Instagram (among many others) will prove useful resources well before you can get your new company off the ground.

Early work and the niche's recognition

Of all the social networking resources at the fingertips of a home-based company owner, popular trends and search functionality are the ones frequently missed the most.

These tools will prove incredibly useful in helping you find a target market that would be lucrative well before you even start a dropshipping company, recognize who your main customers are, and how you can better offer those customers what they want.

As the organization which essentially pioneered the definition of trending trends, Twitter is the perfect forum for people to listen to discussions about the niche within which you want to sell.

For e.g., let's assume that you're talking about starting a clothing company online. Trending subjects, events, and search apps from Twitter will help you discover the kinds of designs and garments most in demand. Of course, this kind of knowledge will be useful when determining which dropship wholesalers to associate with and which lines to buy when you finally set up your online boutique.

These resources may also be used to learn what consumers are thinking about related firms.

Be sure to raise important questions while listening to Twitter discussions regarding your niche, like:

- What do buyers feel in the shops they're shopping at right now?

- How do I imitate the likable elements in my own company that will help me make money dropshipping?

- What's it that clients don't like? What will I avoid?

- What consumers do not get from established online retailers that I can supply to them, thereby building my own niche market and establishing a special, marketable brand in what may already be a highly competitive space?

You are of course not restricted to Twitter alone. Yahoo, Instagram, Pinterest, Tumblr, Twitter, and dozens of other social networking marketing platforms all have search features and can be used to help you develop a successful campaign for your new shop.

Things to Avoid in Your Social Media Dropshipping Business

No Uniqueness

One explanation for a weak response to your marketing strategy for Social Media may be that you don't provide anything special or worth checking out to the clients. Keep this in mind that many of the dropshipping distributors may be offering the very same items you offer.

It's usually not a problem to offer the same goods as other companies as long as you make the ads exclusive so that your items and advertisement stand out from the rest.

Irregularity in posting content

Another problem with your approach might be that you don't regularly post material to your site. You need a regular posting schedule and you'll need to write regularly.

Simply stated, if you want the items to have more fans and more audiences, you need to be quite consistent with it. Irregularity may be a factor why Social Media might not function as a marketing strategy.

Not Publicly accessible

You should never hold a private account of your company. You can use your private account as you like, but having your business account unavailable to the public can never generate profits with your company dropshipping.

So make sure your company pages on Social Media are still available.

Lack of interaction

The more involved you are on your corporate social media accounts, the better for your company. You need to interact with your customers and prospects so that they always have positive interactions and keep building your partnership with them. Posting pictures just won't do – you ought to represent your clients well.

Remember that it is the most important thing.

Not Using Hashtags Properly

If you are not making use of hashtags properly, then you're not maximizing your social media reach. There are several cases in which the usage of acceptable hashtags has proved to be a tremendous value to companies.

For e.g., Samsung teamed up with five Prominent Instagrammers who were using the Samsung Galaxy Note. They used the #benoteworthy hashtag to create a powerful Instagram campaign which left a mark on the minds of the people.

Tips for Refining the Corporate Communications Plan for Social Networking

Using Correct Hashtags

Data reveals that articles without hashtags receive more attention than tweets without hashtags. Using hashtags (and, most specifically, the correct ones) will also render the goods even more accessible to the target audience.

Just attach a simple caption and a few hashtags to any posts that you make. Such hashtags categorize the images and videos, which makes editing them simpler.

Use the correct hashtags will be a tremendous value to your activities on social media. But it won't really do just add some crazy hashtag at the end of the message. And wisely pick the hashtags.

Below are few tips for utilizing hashtags in the strongest possible way:

- You have to have your hashtags related to the content.
- Check to find which hashtags the rivals made use of.
- Use hashtags to match your image.
- Start creating your own sponsored hashtags.
- Allow the widest possible usage of social networking resources.

There are various platforms for social networking that can be used to automate marketing activities because it encourages people to contact, call, or text the company. You clearly need to move from your personal account to a business account, as company profiles offer you access to perspectives and promotional capacity.

Nice Images

When you want the consumers to quickly remember your name, you need to focus on the graphics that you are using. Only inserting photos wouldn't perform as well so getting them visible is key.

This can be achieved through:

- Filters are used to generate clearer visuals.

- Seek to keep up with the hue and design theme.

- More critical than quantities is the consistency of the visuals.

- The captions surrounding the graphics shouldn't be too many to mask the visual effect.

Embrace Yourself

The most critical move, I'd imagine, is becoming acquainted with the customers.

If you're involved in social media your fans will notice you. Just as relevant though you want to collaborate with and get more visibility through regular engagement with friends, blogs, and publishing networks. If you expect someone to follow your material, so you will have to obey their material.

Create a Brand Name for Your Username

While this might not always be feasible, to be more accurate, you can make your username the same as your brand name. Seek to stop saying 'a,' 'the,' 'the' before the company name to opt with the name itself right away.

Taking Measures When the Time Is right

It can be a blessing for your company to publish the content while consumers are more involved. Posting can also create more communication and conversations with your fans during peak usage hours.

Eventually, the success of your social networking activities, and eventually the effects it has on your views and revenue, would be directly related to how dedicated you are to sharing and engaging daily.

Therefore, if you want to optimize the amount of social media traffic and sales, make sure you publish on a regular and consistent schedule. Make sure you get out there too and spend time building relationships and interactions with your audience in quality.

Shopify with Social Media

Despite its easy but powerful functionality, Shopify is slowly becoming a common forum for developing your e-store. This allows you to create an online store, control your goods, market them, and monitor your earnings. Shopify offers four main features that take care of your business from the very start. It offers a comprehensive e-commerce solution that lets you keep everything you want.

1. Front of the store:

Besides the attractive designs, there are many essential features the storefront wants to run successfully in a competitive market. Best Shopify themes crafted by experts attract your store. You can easily modify every design to add a unique look to your store. Customize your store to add an essential feature that will give you an immense advantage.

Every e-commerce prototype is mobile-friendly, so you can sell your goods on any smartphone. This will also boost the image of your brand and your network of customers. To build a beautiful storefront, Shopify offers you the best feature. By supplying you with a full blogging forum, it means you are publishing valuable knowledge regarding your company and keeping your user involved with business ideas.

An HTML and CSS access allows you to customize the store whenever you wish. This choice is really beneficial if various parts of your shop need to be changed.

2. Wagon shopping:

There are major roles you need to remember when it comes to the shopping cart. Security comes first on the list as visitors always have doubts about making a purchase online. Each e-store on Shopify is protected by the 256-bit SSL certificate, the level of security that banks use.

Transaction gateways are another important aspect and will meet sellers' criteria for a seamless transaction to be accepted. Shopify has developed nearly 100 gateways of payment to give complete independence when choosing their preferred ones.

When you are working with a multinational company, languages may be a hurdle that reduces your profits. With Shopify, converting your store themes into multiple languages will help you prevent this issue.

Shopify gives you an alternative to reclaim discarded carts. This helps you to send discount emails to individual consumers who abandoned the cart with no transactions. This is an awesome feature and will improve your sale by returning your existing customers.

3. Managing the store:

Shopify's store management is an easy process because you'll get full detail on the customers and their interests. When you have useful info, you won't consider it difficult to organize things.

For every, the income growing function is added. You'll get an opportunity to build consumer profiles that promote the selling of your items. Getting information about your network of consumers helps you deliver better service. Depending on your purchasing experience, place, and more, you'll get a list of customers.

4. SEO and Marketing:

Nobody can ignore the value of advertisement and SEO as long as it affects online sales. Shopify guarantees the shop with its publicity and SEO tactics get a higher profile and traffic. Hire Shopify developers who better understand different features than others, and use the best features for your project.

You will improve the popularity of your shop by utilizing Search Engine Optimization (SEO) so that customers can quickly figure you out. You should rely on just a few important SEO considerations such as tag H1, description, and meta tags.

This creates the shop sitemap.xml. The sitemap has a few tasks to perform to earn a decent place on the search engine result list. It makes your products, web pages, and blog posts understand by a search engine.

If you look from a marketing angle, you need to find promotions for your company and promo coupons. Prepare a bargain for offering faithful customer discounts. It improves your values for the brand.

Everything is really feasible without a social network. Social networking is no longer a venue for a social gathering; instead, it is a rising commercial sector. To boost sales of your products, Shopify connects the shop with Facebook, Twitter, Linked, and other names. It's the location where you can communicate directly with the customers.

For creating an online marketplace, Shopify has been receiving more publicity than others. The amount of functions it provides is immense. You can handle your shop, test your SEO plan, and move your marketing campaign forward. Make your concept appealing to the customers and arrange the way buyers want your goods.

Using Social Media to Drive further Sales in Shopify

There's a whole host of ways for your e-commerce business to generate sales. You may be trying to push traffic-targeted paying advertising, or you may be using SEO to help people find the things they need directly from search engines. Finally, you may suggest creating a social marketing strategy for Shopify to reach new markets, create more revenue, and expand your company.

But it does require a whole strategy to sell on social. You have to do more than just link to your Shopify store and ask people to purchase from you. It's not as hard though as you would initially imagine.

You'll learn here:

- Why social sales lets you find untapped audiences
- What social apps can you use to improve sales to your Shopify store?

- How to use influencer marketing with success to increase your social reach

- The motives for selling a story, and not just a commodity.

Let's just plunge in!

Store Web Technologies

There is a range of Shopify apps that allow you to expand and improve the ways you sell to your social media customers.

Soldsie is a Shopify plugin that allows you to keep track of the sales you produce, your stock, and your Shopify results, even though you sell on a social networking site.

To further support you, this app lets your customers check out on their own checkout page, keeping your branding consistent throughout the entire purchase process.

Shop off devices for social media marketing.

But that is not stopping there. To find the perfect one for your business, have a look at the wide variety of social media apps for Shopify stores.

Marketing Influencer

There are people out there who make up their entire business model through social networks. Often they have followers who reach the 10's if not the 100's of thousands. We already have millions of fans in many instances.

Building a large suite of highly engaged social media followers takes hard work and time, there are no short cuts. But every platform has a large audience and just because your social channels aren't as developed as you would like them to be doesn't mean you can't reach a wide group of potential customers.

Using Influencer marketing you will tap into this crowd.

Influencer marketing is an effective social media strategy for Shopify as it allows you to reap the benefits of social media, even if you have not had the opportunity to build up your own follow-ups.

Influencer marketing operates by charging an influencer to promote the goods on their social media (someone with a larger network presence than you).

There are ways to play the method, though, and if it's anything you like to do, make sure to test through and every influencer you meet and track.

You are searching for the following when doing such evaluations:

- If the market you're aiming to target is close to their fans and brand.

- How much achievement they are getting.

You want to make sure the intentions are matched as to importance. If you sell fishing items, showcasing your goods on an Instagram focusing on beauty products does not make sense for you.

But relying on a social platform that highlights the best locations to go fishing, would make sense.

Likewise, you don't really have to go for the account with the largest following when it comes to reaching it. Using the same case.

Moving for a fishery influencer who has 3,000 active followers is safer than a fashion influencer who has 3 million active followers.

A recent report by Buffer highlighted the cost of using influencer marketing. You are going to pay about $10 for 1000 fans, as you can see.

And you also want to make sure you have the correct sort of followers for the user you want to use to ensure you get the best ROI on your investment.

Untapped Audiences

Too many customers are conscious of the stores? If you operate a relatively new store in Shopify the result is possibly not many. Even if you're established, the potential is always there to reach a wider audience.

Whatever promotional tactics you use within your Shopify store, you want to make sure that you try to reach as many people as possible.

You get access to each person on the network relevant to your niche when you begin selling on social.

If you sell skincare, for example, you could want to create a group of followers who are actively involved in their skincare routines.

People sometimes see your goods on their social media before they would have heard of you. They see the goods and companies in serious situations before they even realized they needed them.

You are able to approach individuals organically in these circumstances that maybe future customers.

Sell a Tale and Not a Product

Although users are willing to follow products on social media, you need to consider what kind of content you are going to share. When you head for the hard sell, you are going to achieve the reverse of driving revenue, you are going to scare away future buyers. If you use social networks to market a message and not the goods, you will prevent such social networking errors.

But what does this signify?

Well, anytime you choose to view high-quality photos of your goods coupled with thought-inducing captions, your product listing pages are fantastic. Nevertheless, the media networks can be used to create a network and provoke a dialogue with the clients and prospective customers.

For example, you want to make sure you have excellent product photography on a visual social channel like Instagram but don't limit yourself to just taking a photo of your product with a plain background.

Alternatively, demonstrate how you use the company in everyday life. These kinds of images are better storytellers than just using pictures of your products.

A clothes company Chubbies uses Instagram to boost revenue and amuse its crowd.

Instagram Page Chubbies

They have over 400,000 fans and you can find in their photos that they don't aim for the hard sell. Instead, they are focusing on the brand and making enjoyable, sharing-worthy content that their consumers enjoy.

Here the use of memes works well because Chubbies has a solid understanding of their brand and what their customers enjoy online consumption.

If your e-commerce shop offers items that fall on the spectrums bad side, the approach that does not work for you.

It's just about knowing who the clients are and building a narrative that truly resonates with them on social media.

One of the main advantages of utilizing Shopify is the plethora of applications that they have at your fingertips to help you expand your company as you wish.

What's more, you'll gain exposure to a brand new untapped market as you start utilizing these devices and create viral traffic that may not have reached you before.

But to make social marketing a success you need to think hard about why people use social media and what type of buyers you're trying to draw.

It all boils down to making sure that you're not only marketing your goods through your social media but rather telling a story.

Conclusion

To those trying to increase their online visibility and profits, social media marketing (SMM) appears to be the new buzz term, but is it all cracked up to be?

S.M.M. businesses are already springing up all over the world these days and reminding everyone who is willing to listen about how extremely relevant social platforms such as Twitter and YouTube are to the company but, for the ordinary small to medium-sized enterprise, can exposure through social networks actually match up to all the hype? Is it really worthwhile investing a small fortune recruiting an SMM company? So has anyone really done their homework on this before recruiting anyone to set up the Facebook company page there? Many SMM businesses set up company sites on Facebook (which are free) for $600 to $1,000 or more and inform their customers they don't need a platform since Facebook is the world's largest social network because everybody has a Facebook account. Now while it may be true that Facebook is the world's largest social network and yes, the members of Facebook are potential consumers, the real question is whether they actually buy? Social networking advertisement firms are all too eager to find out the good benefits of social media, such as how many users are utilizing Facebook or how many messages were sent last year and how many people are watching YouTube videos, etc. I once sat at a company conference next to an SMM "expert" who was sprucing at everyone who came to earshot about the awesome benefits of setting up a Facebook business page for small business (with him, of course) and advertising it on eBay. And, fascinated by the above "expert" suggestions, I looked at him on Facebook only to discover that he had just 11 (not a good start) Facebook followers. So being the study nerd that I am, I wanted to have a closer look at SMM when it came to sales and see how it really succeeded, who does it work for, and why does it succeed for them in social network marketing? And should businesses rely on social networks so heavily for sales?

As a web developer, I was constantly (and increasingly) confronted with a number of social networking challenges when potential customers would say that having a website sounds good but they had a Facebook business page and had been told by various sources (the ever-present but anonymous "they") that social networks were the thing to do, but after discussing their needs it became quite clear that it was the most important thing. I always recommended building a quality website for small and medium-sized enterprises over any type of social network, why? Okay, it's pretty easy since social networking is social media and social networks are not corporate media and business networks (which should be something like LinkedIn). I know that sounds simple but it's true and it's backed up by the statistics. The fact is that social media marketing doesn't tell you that Facebook is a social network, not a search engine, and despite the number of Facebook users and Google users being around the same, people don't use Facebook the same way they use a search engine like Google (which has about half the search engine market), Yahoo and Bing to search for business or products. They use it to stay in touch with friends and family or for news and entertainment. In a recent study conducted by the IBM Center for Market Interest, about 55 percent of all social media consumers said they do not communicate with brands on social media at all and just about 23 percent actively use social media intentionally to connect with brands. Now out of all the people who use social media and interact with brands intentionally or not, the majority (66 percent) say they need to hear a business interacting sincerely before they connect with each other.

And how do you find ads for social media? So is it worth the effort?

Okay, first of all, I'd say that having a well-optimized website will still get you far more business than social media in most cases, especially if you're a small to medium-sized local business because far more users can access a search engine like Google, Yahoo and Bing in "hairdresser Port Macquarie" than they will ever have on any social media site even if you don't have a web site Given all the (not so nice) numbers, though, I do believe company always has a decent opportunity to use social networking but not in the same manner as other SMM practitioners are now, Why? Quite obviously, this does not work in the way they say it does. Basically, SMM Companies and Business as a whole looked at social networks such as Facebook as a fresh market for picking and when Facebook started getting users measured by the million PayPal co-founder Peter Thiel invested US$ 500,000 for 7 percent of the company (in June 2004) and since they made investments in Facebook by a few venture capital firms and in October 2007, Microsoft annually invested in Facebook. Since the early origins of Facebook so far (2012), however, all SMM Corporations and industries have struggled to leverage a large number of online Facebook users. The reality is that percentages don't match consumers. Is it in the best interest of a social media marketing agency to talk up social networks? Definitely. Truly. Is it in the best interests of people in a social network like Facebook to believe that firms can sell en masse through advertising and marketing with them? Obviously, it is. In early 2012, Facebook revealed that its profits in the previous year had jumped 65 percent to $1 billion, as its revenue, mainly from advertising, had jumped nearly 90 percent to $3.71 billion, so clearly, the SMM concept works out for them, but it works out for you? Statistically, no, but it doesn't automatically imply it'll never happen.

I assume the major disparity between social networks and search engines is deliberate. People who use Google are actively searching for things and whether they are performing a hairdresser quest that's what they're searching for at the specific moment. For anything like Facebook, the primary purpose is typically to communicate with friends and relatives. Mark Zuckerberg himself said in October 2008, "I don't think social networks can be monetized in the same way that search (Search Engines) did ... in three years we've got to figure out what the optimum model is. But that's not our main focus today." Perception is one of the biggest issues business is facing with social networks and SMM. According to the IBM Center for

Market Interest research, there were "major differences in what companies believe customers care about and what customers claim they expect from their social networking experiences with companies." For example, people in today's culture don't only want to send you tips, Facebook likes, feedback, or information without having anything back to them, so don't worry. And the primary reason most users offer on social media for engaging with brands or companies is to collect promotions, but the brands and companies themselves believe that the key reason customers connect with them on social media is to hear about new goods. Receiving promotions for companies and corporations places just 12th in their chart of factors why consumers engage with them. Most companies believe that social media will increase advocacy, but only 38 percent of consumers are in agreement.

If companies want to see some sort of result from it, they need to find more innovative ways to connect with social media. In the IBM study of firms that had some form of perspective on how to use social media to their advantage, there were some positive measures seen, bearing in mind that when questioned what they do when engaging with businesses or brands through social media, consumers mention "having deals or promotions" and "buying products and services" as the top two behaviors, both a U.S. ice formation. Alternatively, there is a great program called Twelpforce launched by Best Buys in the U.S., where employees can answer customer questions via Twitter. In both Cold Stone Creamery and Twelpforce, the profit is obviously in the prospective customer's favor, and the perfect secret for social media marketing is to promote without selling (or appearing like your selling), but most social media marketing is oriented on the wrong direction.

Creating a concrete customer interaction user via social networking is not a simple feat and perhaps the main benefit for a company to use social media to improve Google rankings on their websites. Yet the company has to realize that you can't just set up a business profile on Twitter and hope for the best. SMM requires effort, so potential customers need to see merit in what they have to sell in their social media efforts to show them something worth their social interaction and attention, and then greater results can be achieved.

CPSIA information can be obtained
at www.ICGtesting.com
Printed in the USA
LVHW051034141220
674112LV00015B/580